archi
tects
on archi
tects

T0345672

HIRMER

Edited by Dietrich Fink, Uta Graff, Nils Rostek and Julian Wagner

Prologue

by
Dietrich Fink
Uta Graff

Paideia is a central value concept of ancient culture, which understands education in the sense of being influenced by role models. The key elements of this are people and ideas whose impact on others lies in their exemplary nature.

Everyone who devises or produces artifacts is driven by the questions of what he or she draws from and what forces affect the decision of form. Even if every possible answer to these questions possesses an aspect of inscrutability, it is nevertheless necessary to ask them. How do recorded memories articulate themselves in the process of creation? What is one's own process and where does it begin? What must be overcome in order to get to something new? Is there any influence from role models? And does this lie in a person's approach or as a reference in the work? How much space does the influence of this role model occupy? And at what point is it necessary to overthrow this to give one's own vision space.

We are convinced that it is beneficial to occupy oneself with these questions in the process of designing, knowing however that the answers cannot lie in unambiguousness, but rather should strengthen the individuality of each design.

The confrontation with a person and his or her work is always the differentiated reflection of values that are already laid out in oneself. Seen from the present, it is the cross-generational relevance of themes, positions and concepts from previous generations of architects and the question of their transfer into the present.

The texts presented here emerged from dialogues between architects and personalities from the history and theory of architecture, curatorial practice and fine arts. The texts are, through their thematic and argumentative diversity, equally contemporary testimonies and architectural tools.

Readings
of Architecture
by
Mauro Marzo

In his lecture, Mauro Marzo examines the relationship between architects and their references. In doing so, he establishes a connection
between rediscovery, personal reflection and
interpretation as well as elective affinities with
previous generations.

If the rediscovery, in the time between the 1960s and the 1980s, of certain architects who had been forgotten by historiography belongs to the interpretative readings conducted by designers or is the result of research carried out by historians of architecture is a vexata quaestio with which we are often confronted in a university environment.[1] Determining to what extent the process of rediscovering figures set aside by history is attributable to one's own studies, to the investigations of others or to a combination of the two is beyond both the focus of this paper and my expertise. It is, however, of some use to recall the time frame indicated above and the cultural climate in which, for a number of complex reasons, architects began to look with an interest that I would call "operational" at the work done by other architects from the more or less recent past.

Aldo Rossi's essay on Ètienne-Louis Boullée from 1967, written to introduce the Italian translation of *Architecture. Essai sur l'art*,[2] and Giorgio Grassi's essay on Heinrich Tessenow from 1974, which introduces the Italian translation of *Die Architektur der Großstadt*,[3] are far more than the results of a revaluation of two forgotten architects. Instead, they are the results of an analysis that aims at uncovering the operation of architectural design. In this respect, the persistently topical nature of these writings still drives us today to consider them an unavoidable point of reference for those approaching the study of Boullée or Tessenow. Assuming, of course, that the reader's interest is that of a designer and not of a historian.

Boullée's emphasis on rationality and Tessenow's strict compositions were the subjects of Rossi's and Grassi's studies. They were concerned with the design and mediation of the projects, not in order to put unpublished works and those discovered in the archives into print, but out of a conviction that the French and German masters could be useful for their own work as designers.
At a time when a process of true disciplinary refoundation of architecture was emerging, both were instrumental in developing a different approach to design.
To say that Rossi or Grassi identified ideal interlocutors or distant masters in such figures is both vague and reductive. I think it is more useful to underline how, by tendentiously studying these architects, they were interested in deepening questions

related to architectural design. This is, in fact, what Rossi writes at the beginning of his introductory text to *Architecture. Essai sur l'art*: "This essay by Boullée is of particular interest to those who today are convinced of the need for a reading of architecture based on logical principles and argue that architectural design can be based, for the most part, on the development of a series of propositions. Boullée is a rationalist architect in the sense that, having built up a logical system of architecture, he aims to continuously identify the different projects with the assumed principles." [4]

By investigating the architectural and theoretical work of these masters, Rossi and Grassi intended to discover their own way of making architecture in depth and tendentiously take on the points of view of designers who, although they lived in other eras and in other cultural contexts, nevertheless could be perceived as similar.

Starting from the production of writings by architects on other architects over that period of time, and in the face of today's publishing landscape overflowing with monographs on architects, which are often highly valuable but written mostly by non-designers, I think it is necessary to emphasize the importance of these two essays and, more generally, of a broader line of research that makes a significant contribution to working on architectural projects.

Alongside the books full of footnotes and scholarly bibliographies, what designers are increasingly missing are writings that help them understand what, beyond fashions, linguistic figures or correct temporal successions, constitutes the topicality of some designers of the past or even the value of some contemporary designers.

An architect's work draws on knowledge that is differently organized than that of historians. If, for historians, the understanding of events in their exact chronological sequence is an essential question for the investigation of facts, for architects the construction of knowledge follows very different paths [5] and is completely unrelated to the historiographic instruments.

Reading what designers write about the work of other architects, whether contemporary or from the past, allows us to interpret their work from the specific point of view of those who, in professional studios, design and create works and, in universities, teach how to design them. Take, for example, when Peter Eisenman writes about Giuseppe Terragni;[6] when Alberto Campo Baeza writes about Alejandro de la Sota;[7] when Antonio Monestiroli writes about Mies van der Rohe,[8] about Palladio[9] or about Aldo Rossi;[10] when Rafael Moneo writes about the same Eisenman or Rossi, about Álvaro Siza or about James Stirling;[11] or when Alberto Ferlenga writes about Dimitris Pikionis.[12] They reason about the work of these architects taking, in their readings, the specific point of view that derives from their identity as designers.

If this activity of interpretative reading of the works of other architects has taken on a substantially valuable direction in a historical period of disciplinary refounding, what we need to ask ourselves is whether there is, in other artistic fields, something comparable to this activity. Is this an activity that is still active or on the verge of extinction, and does the potential decrease in attention paid to those elective affinities, which each architect can identify in his or her approach to other designers, constitute a weakening of the culture linked to our profession?

There are many examples of writers, sculptors, painters or directors who, in investigating the meaning and techniques of their own research, refer to what has been carried out by other artists. It is enough here to mention only a few figures among the many possible. Giorgio Bassani was one of the most important Italian writers of the twentieth century. The author of *Il giardino dei Finzi-Contini* and many other works set in the city of Ferrara, he has repeatedly declared his cultural debt to Alessandro Manzoni and Marcel Proust. Felice Casorati was part of the pictorial magic realism movement, yet his work cannot be understood without looking at the sharp compositions of Piero della Francesca. In 1978, Jean-Luc Godard was invited to participate in an initiative at the Conservatory of Film Art in Montreal[13] with the request to talk about the history of cinema in a series of seminars. Godard responded to the invitation by proposing to the director of the Conservatory to co-produce a screenplay for which he wanted to use not only written texts but also images and sounds. The idea was to talk about the work of fellow directors through the tools of his own work. If we reflect on this aspect, we realize that it is something very close to the interpretative drawings of the Casa del Fascio and the Palazzina del Girasole made by Eisenman. These drawings are examinations of the most famous work of the Como architect Giuseppe Terragni and a building from Luigi Moretti in Rome, a project also mentioned by Robert Venturi. Ultimately, Godard's method of working is also similar to Moretti's drawings for an essay on Michelangelo's and Borromini's architecture and on Baroque architecture in general, and on the nature of architecture and the possibility of a new architectural criticism. [14]

Although the project by Godard was not finally realized due to a lack of sufficient funds, the initiative is still remembered thanks to the book *Introduzione alla vera storia del cinema* (*Introduction to a True History of Cinema and Television*), which is divided into seven chapters that are described in the index of the volume as voyages. The book consists of recorded conference texts that have been edited and then published. These voyage chapters are what remains of the idea of producing seven real scripts. In each of these chapters, the French director talks about his own films, comparing them to the work of other directors chosen by him as key characters to narrate a personal vision of the history of cinema and, at the same time, to interpret his own work. Whether he is analyzing a film by Roberto Rossellini or the language of Sergei Michailowitsch Eisenstein, what Godard is always really talking about is his own way of seeing cinema. The critical reading of the work of other directors becomes, in some way, instrumental to his understanding of his own work and its overall meaning. Of course, the history of cinema is a short one when compared to the history of architecture, which covers the entire course of humanity. However, Godard makes full use of this short period: his seven journeys range from the first attempts at film production to the works of the Nouvelle Vague. In each chapter, the director talks with full critical awareness only about himself; the work of the other filmmakers serves in supporting the study of technical and figurative aspects of his own work. This intention was already present in the idea for the seminar in Montreal as well as in the book in which the results are presented. The interpretative readings of the films of other directors become an opportunity to draft a new screenplay that was, in fact, if we want to use a term dear to architects, a project: the project of a film.

When a designer writes about the work of another architect, he makes a highly tendentious reading, like that made by Godard. In fact, there is a sort of cultural, personal and operational necessity that leads the architect to reflect on his work through the work of other architects. This necessity calls for specific hierarchies that are not chronological or linguistic in nature, but are directly related to the imperatives of the trade, the will to face particular problems and the need to answer questions that have to do with the form and character of a project as well as the relationship established with a place or with a specific compositional theme.

In architecture, the range of critical work has not reached a level comparable to that in other artistic fields, for example, in literature, painting, sculpture or music. On the contrary, it can be argued without difficulty that architects, in the course of history, have not frequently written about the work of other architects. It is true that, from the Renaissance onwards, there is hardly a reflection that does not refer to Vitruvius. However, apart from the numerous treatises and manuals, the culture of architects has left a much more limited collection of written evidence than that of other forms of artistic expression.

Nevertheless, as I mentioned, there was a time when this activity took on great importance and influenced a review process that would lead to profound changes in the approach to architectural design. I refer in particular to a period of time, ending in the 1980s, in which Italian architectural culture took a leading role in the evolution of the international architectural debate.

During this period, the magazine *Casabella* became an important platform for discussion and critical examination of designers' projects as well as purely disciplinary matters. From 1953 to 1964, the magazine was under the direction of Ernesto Nathan Rogers. After a period of changing management, Tomás Maldonado took over from 1977 to 1982, followed by Vittorio Gregotti from 1982 to 1996. In particular, it was under the direction of Rogers that the critical interpretation of designers' work became important. Some issues of the magazine are well known and cited precisely because of their focus on almost forgotten architects or because they looked at designers who, sometimes for political reasons, had been removed from the architectural debate: Peter Behrens, Adolf Loos and Auguste Perret, to name a few of the most famous examples. Talking about Behrens in Italy, shortly after the Second World War, was certainly not straightforward. At a time in history when this extraordinary German architect was associated with Nazi culture (whether this association was right or wrong is not clear), dealing with a reinterpretation of his work was a complex matter—all the more so when one thinks that *Casabella* was then under the direction of Rogers, who had suffered in the war years because of his Jewish descent. There was nothing easy or predictable, therefore, in this approach. Yet, Rogers, together with young colleagues who were linked to that magazine—Aldo Rossi, Vittorio Gregotti, Giorgio Grassi and Guido Canella—chose to write about these forgotten or suppressed architects. These cultural strategies were by no means justified by historiographic gaps but were rather dictated by the rethinking of some design issues that had been imposed on the cultural debate in the post-war period and in the years of the so-called economic boom. These issues ranged from the relationship between architecture and the city to the link between design and aspects of construction. In his introduction to Tessenow's book, Grassi is very clear on the subject: "I will immediately say, in order to remove the biggest misunderstandings, that it would be wrong to attribute . . . to the present translation the value of a historical document destined to enrich the cognitive material around a particular moment in the history of European architecture . . . This writing by Tessenow, on the other hand, was translated and published again today, as it represents a profoundly topical lesson in architecture as a whole. . . . In fact, the importance of a specific discourse on architecture and its construction has never been clearer than in recent years." [15]

The extraordinary thing that took place in those years, not only in the editorial staff of *Casabella* but also in other Italian magazines, was the construction of a sort of geography of architectural affinities, configured through discoveries and rediscoveries. [16] The architects I mentioned, generally linked to a modern or immediately pre-modern period, seem to outline in their entirety a different modernity from that illustrated in volumes on the history of architecture written after the war. Of course, some referred their reflections to past epochs, such as the text by Rossi about Boullée mentioned at the beginning. The map of references of these architects was, therefore, not built through chronological successions or stylistic families. It is a geography composed of personalities from architecture who often had little to do with each other, and whose rediscovery can now be understood only by considering the points of view of those who faced the study. There was no objectivity in those choices; subjective interests, shared cultural strategies and clearly taken positions led to the rediscovery of a certain architect rather than another.

Naturally, I don't think that the interpretation of an architect's work by another is a purely Italian phenomenon, nor that it only took place in that historical moment. I have already mentioned Eisenman's analysis of Terragni's work, an interpretation of the work of the Lombard architect far removed from that to be found in historical monographs. Eisenman allows us to look at Terragni through the syntactic-formal approach that characterizes Terragni's entire production.

Another extraordinary reading, which, unlike that of Eisenman, is less influenced by the Italian debate, is the story of the construction of the abbey of Le Thoronet, in the South of France, by the architect Fernand Pouillon. The book he published in 1964, *Les Pierres sauvages*,[17] was written as an imaginary diary of the anonymous architect and builder of the abbey. There is a sort of inevitable identification between Pouillon and the architect of the past, a convergence on choices, a correspondence between gestures that have been repeated over time and refer to a number of unchangeable conditions. We do not know who this architect actually was; nevertheless, Le Corbusier, and later Fernand Pouillon, devoted deep thought to this architectural complex. And there is also, to be comprehensive, a more recent text by Eduardo Souto de Moura [18] in which the events of the abbey are the subject of some observations— needless to say, once again determined by the assumption of a point of view that is not historical but a creative concern.

This panorama of readings by designers on the work of other architects outlines a sort of landscape parallel to that of official historiography. The famous text by Grassi on Tessenow has not only the merit of bringing an architect, in whom nobody seemed to be interested at that time, out of Italian oblivion, but has also certainly influenced the attention of architectural historians and led to a number of clarifications. The archival documents were analyzed and studied and led to the production of essays and monographs. But it was precisely Grassi's artistically intended and strategic view that drew attention to Tessenow again, at least in Italy. The deep connection between the Italian architect and the German architect stimulated reflections on the elementary observations on buildings in which Tessenow was a master.

An architect who talks about another architect is certainly biased. His interest in dealing with the work of a particular architect is the search for possible answers to questions that he asks himself anew every day. For this reason, it may happen that his reading differs from the historical truth, and he may, perhaps unjustly, be accused by architectural historians of a misinterpretation that could lead to misunderstandings and could remove the work under consideration from the context of social, economic and cultural realities, as well as in relation to the client. However, it would be legitimate to ask oneself if historical truth is all that matters? And what historical truth? Eisenman's interpretation of Terragni's Casa del Fascio is certainly very far from the documented and archived reality, but, at the same time, it appears incredibly close to the design thinking of the American architect. It offers us an interpretative key for understanding not only the Como master but the design thinking of Eisenman himself. He finds in Terragni what he was looking for on his personal path as a designer. The same applies to Aldo Rossi with regard to Adolf Loos, [19] thanks to whose work he was able to develop his own vision of architecture. It is the critically interpretive and yet completely subjective aspect that makes both readings interesting.
Despite the great importance that is still given to these readings today, the cultural framework that I have roughly sketched in the previous pages has been completely transformed, and the reasons that had given substance to those interpretative actions have been completely exhausted. Few architects still practise this way of studying and researching, and they derive to some extent, directly or indirectly, from the context I have described. My impression is that this interpretative activity, carried out

by designers on the work of other architects, has been com-
promised by an increasing form of specialism. This is particularly true in Italy, but it is not only there; perhaps it is a much
more widespread phenomenon. Historians, critics and designers have skills that now appear independently of one another
and without overlapping points in almost all areas.

This has certainly made it possible to further develop strictly disciplinary knowledge and, at the same time, to divide up
fields of competence whose origins are unitary. It was the unitary nature of this knowledge that made the flourishing of the
architectural debate described here possible; a debate that does
not refer to history, or to architectural criticism, but to something different. Specifically, it refers to the way in which architects engaged in the project were building their own culture—a
culture that is not fixed and changes relentlessly over time, that
is always subjective and deliberately biased, and that, above
all, should be constantly nourished with new readings that are
inclined to specific points of view. The greatest risk we run lies
not only in the exhaustion of this culture but principally in the
loss of critical awareness of the profound reasons for our own
discipline.

1   One of these opportunities was the talk "Architects Talk about
Architects" ("Architetti che parlano di architetti") between Marco
Biraghi, Alberto Ferlenga and Antonio Monestiroli, which was moder-
ated by Mauro Marzo, on 6 June 2013 at the Scuola di Dottorato of the
IUAV University of Venice, in the Sala del Consiglio in Palazzo Badoer,
Venice.
2   Aldo Rossi, "Introduction to Boullée", in Ètienne-Louis Boullée,
Architecture. Essay on Art, ed. Alberto Ferlenga (Turin: Einaudi, 2005),
XXIII–XLIII.
3   Giorgio Grassi, "L'architettura come mestiere" ("Introduction
to H. Tessenow") in *Heinrich Tessenow, Osservazioni elementari sul*

costruire (*Elementary Observations about Building*) (Milan: Giorgio Grassi, Franco Angeli, 1989), 21–68.

4   Aldo Rossi, "Introduction to Boullée", in Ètienne-Louis Boullée, *Architecture. Essay on Art*, ed. Alberto Ferlenga (Turin: Einaudi, 2005), XXIII.

5   Cf. Paolo Rossi, "Scienze della natura e scienze umane: la dimenticanza e la memoria", *Casabella*, 577 (March 1991), 39–41.

6   Peter Eisenman, *Giuseppe Terragni: trasformazioni, scomposizioni, critiche*, with texts by Giuseppe Terragni and Manfredo Tafuri (Macerata: Quodlibet, 2004).

7   Alberto Campo Baeza, *Laconico Sota* (Syracuse: LetteraVentidue, 2017).

8   Antonio Monestiroli, "Le forme e il tempo", in Ludwig Hilberseimer, *Mies van der Rohe* (Turin: CittàStudiEdizioni, 1993), 7–17.

9   Id., *In compagnia di Palladio* (Syracuse: LetteraVentidue, 2013).

10   Id., *Il mondo di Aldo Rossi* (Syracuse: LetteraVentidue, 2015).

11   Rafael Moneo, *Inquietudine teorica e strategia progettuale nell'opera di otto architetti contemporanei* (Milan: Electa, 2005).

12   Alberto Ferlenga, *Pikionis. 1887–1968* (Milan: Electa, 1999); id., *Le strade di Pikionis* (Syracuse: LetteraVentidue, 2014).

13   See Jean-Luc Godard, *Introduzione alla vera storia del cinema* (*Introduction to the True History of Cinema and Television*) (Milan: Pgreco, 2012) IX–XII. I am indebted to Alberto Ferlenga for the reference to this book by the French director and for several other ideas expressed in this paper.

14   Cecilia Rostagni, "Moretti, Michelangelo e il barocco", in *Casabella*, 745 (June 2006), 81–85.

15   Giorgio Grassi, "L'architettura come mestiere", in *Casabella*, 745 (June 2006), 21–22.

16   About the magazine *Lotus international*, see Mauro Marzo, "Lotus. I primi trent'anni di una rivista di architettura"/"Lotus. The first thirty years of an architectural magazine", monographic issue of the online magazine (It./En.), in *Festival dell'Architettura*, 43 (March–April 2014), 41-66, http://www.famagazine.it/index.php/famagazine/article/view/142/681

17   Fernand Pouillon, *Les Pierres sauvages* (Paris: Éditions du Seuil, 1964).

18   Dominique Machabert, Eduardo Souto de Moura, *Eduardo Souto de Moura. Au Thoronet, le diable m'a dit...* (Marseille: Parenthèses, 2012).

19   Aldo Rossi, "Adolf Loos, 1870–1933", in *Casabella-Continuità*, 233 (November 1959), 5–12.

Mauro Marzo was born in Catania in 1968. He is Associate Professor in Architecture and Urban Design at the IUAV University of Venice and is a member of the Architectural Composition Curriculum Board at the IUAV PhD School. He was also adjunct professor at the University of Parma and the Bochum University of Applied Sciences. He is co-founder and coordinator of the international network of architecture schools "Designing Heritage Tourism Landscapes", director of the monograph series *Figure* by LetteraVentidue and editor of the *FAMagazine*. He was a member of the Italian National University Council from 2017 to 2019, and since 2018 he has been President's Delegate for Teaching.

Arno Lederer
on Sigurd Lewerentz
with
Philip Ursprung

When Arno Lederer and Philip Ursprung meet, a
conversation develops around Sigurd Lewerentz
that covers a wide range of topics, from memory
and perception to learning itself.

AL How did this constellation come about: Lewerentz, Ursprung and me?

PU I can't tell you. I wasn't allowed to choose.

AL I simply agreed, to Sigurd Lewerentz and to you—and I didn't think about it any further.

PU Neither did I. I'm not a Sigurd Lewerentz expert, and we both haven't met before.

AL Those are good prerequisites.

PU You started studying architecture in Stuttgart in 1969 and went to Vienna in 1975.

AL Yes, that's true. I always wanted to become an architect, and I think one studies architecture for the very banal reason of wanting to build beautiful houses. I don't think there is any other reason. Of course, architecture also has something to do with art, so you think about studying art right away. "But with architecture," parents always say, "you can at least earn a little money." And that's why I chose architecture. However, the concept of beauty was driven out during my studies. The message was rather: architecture has nothing to do with beauty—and nothing to do with art. The Left has always said that architecture will soon no longer exist anyway, only large planning offices, i.e. collectives, will exist. If architecture ceases to exist, I thought, then I'll study monument preservation. That's why I went to Vienna and studied this subject there for a year. After that, I knew that I didn't want to work as a monument curator, so I went back to Stuttgart. However, I have to point out, I didn't learn much during my studies.

PU In one of your books, you start with a quote from Alexander Kluge's film *Artists Under the Big Top: Perplexed* to sum up the mood back then. I have heard similar things from other colleagues who were studying at the same time. Jacques Herzog calls the period between the late 1960s and 1970s the "great emptiness", Peter Zumthor calls it the "caesura" and Peter Märkli calls it the "vacuum". Do you see it the same way?

AL Yes, politically you would say it was an interregnum. Previously, post-war modernism was a predominant school with great reliability. The professors who had learned from the great masters such as Le Corbusier, Walter Gropius or Mies van der Rohe were now only "modern". But, basically, they lacked a classical education. This was a time in which everything had to be horizontal and made of concrete, and in which construction provided the aesthetic expression. This safety was suddenly gone, both in urban planning and in building construction. The 1968 generation questioned for the first time how things really were and what was lost. This, of course, had a major political component, especially in Germany due to the Third Reich.

PU But the 1970s were also the period of recession. I spoke, for example, to Ernst Gisel, who said that the biggest problem was the lack of commissions. In the 1960s, he was able to build half of Berlin and in the 1970s suddenly nothing was available.

AL Yes, that was the oil crisis of 1973. And suddenly the Club of Rome, founded in 1968, entered the public consciousness. That was the first reflection on the meaning and finiteness of resources and creation in the broadest sense. It was also the time when the question of architectural history came up again; a question that until then had no relation at all to design and was completely ignored in the post-war period. In this way, the destruction of cultural things that evoke images and memories that took place in the 1950s can also be understood. Even our teachers' generation did not want to remember at that time.

PU Was this what led you to Ernst Gisel as a young architect?

AL Yes, I worked for him right after my studies. Gisel had built the Sonnenberg Church in Stuttgart, but it didn't touch me much. I had seen the small church of Rigi Kaltbad, in the canton of Lucerne, in a book. I liked this chapel made of plaster and wood, with its round corner and the view into the valley. All the same, I was confounded by the fact that, standing inside on the gallery of this beautiful vantage point, there is no view outside. I could not understand that. How can you build on a mountain and not create any reference to the outside? Since then, Ernst Gisel has interested me. I worked for him for a year and in that year, I learned everything I hadn't learned at university. Although Gisel was authoritarian and strict, he had a certain kindness, and our relationship was very good.

PU So, this church was an aesthetic magnet that attracted you. Was this because there was nothing like it in your architectural environment?

AL The question is why something appeals to you or why not. I think perfection is boring and irritation makes you think. This is the case in art and, of course, in architecture as well. This moment of irritation also exists in that church without a view.

PU The motifs that appear again and again in your work are the staircase turned outwards, the balconies and the curves of the buildings. Are these also indications of irritation?

AL They could be. The question of corporeality and also a certain preference for curves certainly plays an important role for me. That's probably why I enjoyed working with Ernst Gisel so much. It is really hard to make something round. Gisel had an eye for it and he also drew it up. This sketching, seeing how the hand moves the pen, was something very important. Many things don't come from the head but from the hand. You also develop a feeling for grasping, seeing, smelling and feeling very early on. The synaesthetic process of seeing objects, touching them and knowing how they smell makes up the space. These early experiences with material, physicality and light are so formative that they are transferred to one's own work.

PU I find the connection between the sense of touch, synaesthesia and language, which is also related to haptics, highly interesting. Has this connection been driven out of us at school?

AL Absolutely. We are at a point where architecture is changing a lot. Through computers—whose formidable properties cannot be denied—we're seeing the end of doing things by hand. I also believe that in today's educational system, with its emphasis on scientific subjects, there is a loss of thought, imagination and sensitivity. Whether this is for the

Ernst Gisel
Bergkirche
Rigi Kaltbad 1963

Ernst Gisel
Bergkirche
Rigi Kaltbad 1963

better or for the worse, I do not want to judge, but I certainly belong to a generation that embraced the concept of thinking by hand. This connection of body, movement and thinking about material and form is important. We don't invent, we find things. And our hand, which draws something, perhaps even something awkward or comical, actually suggests how it can work.

PU Is that a design methodology of yours?

AL Yes, especially at the beginning of a project. You start drawing, you try to correct it, you draw over and over again and, finally, you think it is wrong. But the hand actually does it correctly. This dialogue between head and hand is essential.

PU In your case, are pictures already present before you start drawing, or do they only appear in the course of time?

AL Unfortunately before, but that's the way it goes for all of us. The flood of images on the Internet is tempting. You think you've found something yourself, but you've just seen it somewhere. On the other hand, it can also happen that too many pictures relativize that again.

PU I'm now thinking about the figure of the stove in the single-family house that you built in the early 1980s. The stove in the niche, with the stacked wood on one side, is a kind of focal point, but at the same time a hinge of the house. The fireplace is an archetype of the stove, something archaic, but at the same time, it is still a contemporary stove. Was there a reference for it before it came into being, or did it just evolve?

AL There was probably such a picture. I would be lying if I said, "I made it up." No, there was certainly a picture, but I don't know which one; it doesn't matter either.
Geoffrey Baker, for example, describes Le Corbusier's sketchbooks as a kind of library. That's because each hand-drawn sketch is also stored in the head, so that the physical sketchbook is not necessarily needed in the design process. Enriching this library of the mind is much more important than learning technical details that are outdated anyway. Antoine de Saint-Exupéry says, "If you want to build a ship, don't drum up

people to collect wood and don't assign them tasks and work, but rather teach them to long for the endless immensity of the sea." In our education, we learn to make boats, but we often don't know what to do with them.

PU You said that you actually learned nothing until you worked for Ernst Gisel. Do you have the feeling that during your studies you learned autodidactically beyond what was offered?

AL Yes, I was able to build my first house as a student. But, basically, I had to work out everything myself. Later, when I was teaching, I became very interested in how to get young people to develop enthusiasm for something and how to explain to them that intrinsic learning is the real goal. Today, there are more and more specialists who tell you how architecture works and, above all, how to measure it quantitatively. But to make something that doesn't just work economically and constructively, but also exists as a place where one likes to be is the great secret and the specific talent of the architect. Unfortunately, this ability is no longer as appreciated and accepted as it used to be. It is an unsatisfying state of affairs that the question of architecture ranks far below the question of economics.

PU Can education change this?

AL Yes, but then we have to change the schoolish system of universities. Students should simply start designing. And when they come to a point where they have to get something, acquire something, then they would need a mentor to help them. Someone who knows where to look or what to do. And this new system would need to include art and architecture history, not chronologically but phenomenologically. The corner conflict existed in antiquity and in the nineteenth century—just like it does today.

PU The idea that the corner conflict occurs in every epoch presupposes that architecture is something continuous.

AL We live in a time of progress; technology is constantly being improved. And one automatically thinks that architecture also has something to do with progress. But that's not true.

Lederer Ragnarsdóttir Oei
House B
Aichwald 1981

There are very few inventions in architectural principles. That's why they differ from technology. Karl Jaspers' *Way to Wisdom: An Introduction to Philosophy* explains that philosophy is not subject to the idea of progress. It is nonsense to say that Peter Sloterdijk is more progressive than Immanuel Kant and that Kant is more progressive than Plato. Just as it is absurd in music to claim that Mozart is more progressive than Bach. And the same applies to architecture.

PU My historical model is also discontinuous. The past has nothing to do with the present by default. Things are disparate, and we construct connections. Perhaps there is also resonance and affinity between certain events. That is why I am more interested in conflicts or differences than in continuity. Are you clear about things that you specifically do not want in your work?

AL Actually not, at least not immediately. I would always first see whether I could use something or not. Of course, there are things that I reject completely without reason.

PU So, the process doesn't work by negation?

AL In the past, that happened more often, but nowadays it is no longer the case. As a young architect, you naturally have an idea of what the enemy is. You need that to set yourself apart. When you get older, you become more relaxed and you know more and understand what you want. But bowing to economy, politics and the often absurd normative guidelines makes me mad. This turns architecture into a technical product and moves a built space away from the possibility of being felt and loved.

PU This is exactly the possibility you want to create with your buildings. In my opinion, your buildings represent the commune, i.e. the area accessible to all, which stands between the private and the public. It is an area that can neither be taken over by private interests nor by the public sector. When you create public buildings, they do not celebrate the transparency popular with the authorities. They are opaque. When did this attraction to Gisel's attitude begin?

AL I don't remember. But Ernst Gisel and Sigurd Lewerentz were the types of architects you actually wanted to become: casual clothes, smoking cigarettes at their desks, in the light of the lamp and with a bottle of port wine in front of them—as the photo of Lewerentz in his office shows. You can feel that he's not just sitting there; he's drawing and he doesn't even notice that he's working. He is in a kind of flow through which he creates things with his hand. This way of working is fascinating because knowledge is created by doing. And, of course, Lewerentz's view of space is also fascinating. For Lewerentz, there is space on the outside, for the public, and space on the inside, for the private. The exciting thing about that is the control of the transition, the precise opening up and the resulting visual relationships between inside and outside. I am also fascinated by Sigurd Lewerentz's studio, which Klas Anshelm planned for him. It was under the roof, and when you entered, you had to bend down because of a beam. Lewerentz kept bumping his head there and although he could have changed it, he never did. It somehow kept him awake. Actually, that's just a banality, but in a way, it's similar to those haptic, early childhood memories that shape you.

> **PU** It certainly also has to do with the question of where architects get their material from, what they draw from. For example, for Jacques Herzog, it is the smell of the school building, and for Peter Zumthor, it is walking through a village. These biographical coincidences, these moments, whether images, music or objects from memory, have a great deal to do with one's own architectural work. Is the brick as material something that connects you and Sigurd Lewerentz?

AL Certainly. I liked the brick church Sankt Petri Kyrka in Klippan, which I first came across in a report about an excursion to Scandinavia by Friedrich Kurrent. That's why I went there. But another aspect that plays an important role for me, as well as for Lewerentz, is the processing of a project until its completion. Not only the drawing but also the observation, participation and co-decision right till the end is a common feature that we share. But in general, there is a lot that connects me with Scandinavian architecture. My wife, Jórunn Ragnarsdóttir, comes from Iceland. And it's not just the works of Sigurd Lewerentz that are important to me, but also those of Peter Celsing and Alvar Aalto, who, by the way, was friends with Ernst Gisel.

PU One of your principles is "First the city, then the house". When I think now of Iceland, I'm surprised you don't say, "First the landscape, then the house". Does landscape play a role for you?

AL Landscape no longer exists in Germany. I would call it a factory, the forest is a factory, the fields and meadows are a factory. In Iceland, there is still landscape. And if someone were to say, build me a church on an Icelandic volcano, then I would immediately agree, but only out of pure egoism. The city itself is the most important thing, and also the most sustainable. But we no longer think about urban space. We only think, at least in southwest Germany, about objects: you build a house and the next architect builds another. All houses are designed as self-referential objects. This, however, makes us lose the feeling for the public space. It is dominated only by infrastructures and individuality. The idea of the identity of the individual house and the distinction between old and new promote this loss of public space. The city is an organism that desperately needs the superordinate. For centuries this has worked quite naturally, simply by continuing to build. The city of the twenty-first century is particularly missing places that are not subject to the economy, to economic coercion. But these are incredibly important places. Churches like the Asamkirche in Munich, for example, where you can quickly escape the hustle and bustle of the city and where it is very dark and quiet. It is a memorable experience that corresponds—in a different spatial way—to what you experience when you enter Sigurd Lewerentz's Chapel of Resurrection at the cemetery in Stockholm. Much more than the use of brick, this spatial understanding connects me with Sigurd Lewerentz.

Sigurd Lewerentz
Chapel of Resurrection
Stockholm 1925

Sigurd Lewerentz
Chapel of Resurrection
Stockholm 1925

Arno Lederer was born in Stuttgart in 1947 and studied architecture at the University of Stuttgart and the Technical University of Vienna. After working for Ernst Gisel and Berger Hauser Oed, he founded his own architectural office in 1979. Since 1985, he has shared an office with Jórunn Ragnarsdóttir; they were joined by Marc Oei in 1992. From 1985 to 1990, Arno Lederer was Professor for Construction and Design at the HFT Stuttgart. In 1990 he took over the Chair for Building Construction and Design I at the University of Karlsruhe, where he also held the Chair for Building Theory and Design from 1997 to 2005. Afterwards, he held the Professorship for Public Building and Design at the University of Stuttgart from 2005 to 2014. Completed work from Lederer Ragnarsdóttir Oei includes administrative and school buildings as well as numerous buildings for the Protestant and Catholic churches and the Art Museum in Ravensburg from 2013.

Philip Ursprung was born in Baltimore in 1963 and studied art history, general history and German literature in Geneva, Vienna and Berlin. After academic positions at the Université de Genève, the Kunsthochschule Berlin-Weissensee, the Hochschule der Künste Berlin, the University of Basel, the University of Zurich, Columbia University and the Barcelona Institute of Architecture, he has been Professor of Art and Architecture History at ETH Zurich since 2011. Since 2017, he has been Dean of the Department of Architecture at ETH Zurich. His publications include *Die Kunst der Gegenwart: 1960 bis heute*, 2010, and *Der Wert der Oberfläche: Essays zu Architektur, Kunst und Ökonomie*, 2018, as author, and *Herzog & de Meuron: Naturgeschichte*, 2002, as editor.

Sigurd Lewerentz was born in Sandö in 1885 and died in Lund in 1975. From 1905 to 1908 he studied architecture at the Chalmers Technical College in Gothenburg. After working with Bruno Möhring in Berlin and with Theodor Fischer and Richard Riemerschmid in Munich, he opened his own office in 1911. In collaboration with Gunnar Asplund, he planned the Stockholm Forest Cemetery from 1914, where he also built the neoclassical Chapel of Resurrection in 1926. Together with Asplund, he was also chief architect of the Stockholm Exhibition in 1930, a national exhibition of modern architecture, design and art. Among his most important works are the Church of St Mark in Stockholm, completed in 1962, and the Church of St Peter in Klippan in 1966.

on Oswald Mathias Ungers

with Jasper Cepl

Hans Kollhoff, a former colleague of Oswald
Mathias Ungers, and Jasper Cepl, Ungers' biog-
rapher, know Ungers and his work well. In their
conversation, they focus on his conceptual approaches and their significance for architec-

HK   Before I start being provocative, I want to say that Oswald Mathias Ungers was my greatest teacher. I had many teachers, but Ungers was by far the most influential. Without Ungers, I wouldn't be Hans Kollhoff. The time in which I worked with him was a very intense period, although I was not working on his buildings myself. In my renewed occupation with these years, it became clear to me, among other things through your book *An Intellectual Biography*, that this conversation should not be about documenting the work of an architect, and certainly not about the buildings per se, but about his thinking.

Now, here's the provocation: when I prepared the lecture on Ungers and went through my countless slides from that time, I said to myself that I should actually finish with a photo of a building by Ungers that I really like. But I couldn't find one.

JC   I'm happy to maintain that level of provocation, and I'm actually not surprised at all. I agree with you that his ideas are the decisive factor. His buildings have never interested me that much, or, let's say, they weren't the reason why I dealt with Ungers.

HK   If you take the idea further, then, of course, you can also ask yourself the question, "Was the architect Ungers interested in building?" I think he wanted to build, but he kept the associated effort off his own back.

JC   I don't think he felt responsible for how they were built. He accepted the conditions of production in their meagreness and tried to get some kind of expression out of them. When one observes how he develops his position and when he, especially at the end of his career, makes these radically geometric buildings, one could find in that the conscious decision of saying, "I am responsible for the form, but the execution is what the building industry supplies. That's not my problem." As a position, I find that unacceptable.

HK   This attitude was already noticeable before he went to America. I remember a lecture by Ungers in which he settles up with the construction situation and complains how miserable it is that there are only speculators left who are not interested in building themselves. To be honest, he was an opportunist in this respect. He wrote that he could not have quit for economic reasons. If you take that as a reason, then an architect can go along with anything.

There has been no fundamental change in the conditions. What has changed is that this period from the late 1960s to the 1990s was a great time for architecture, in which Ungers played an important role internationally. It was a time when architecture came back into people's heads and became a topic again. The result was a multitude of incredibly good publications on architecture. One can list five Italian, four American and three English magazines just off the top of one's head. Only in Germany was and is there nothing comparable, because this country still has to cope with the past. Ungers was the only German to play an important role in this international discussion, an intellectually stimulating and exciting debate that influences me to this day.

JC   We can certainly agree on that. In fact, that's why I also dealt with him. In Germany, there was only Ungers, and then there was nothing for a long time.

But I would like to come back to the question of building. I think there's really a concept in how Ungers ended up dealing with construction. I think this is shown best in a discussion with Léon Krier at a meeting of architects in Charlottesville in 1982.

HK   My friend Léon Krier wiped the floor with him in a most indecent way.

JC   Right. It was about the Torhochhaus of the Frankfurt Fair. Krier accused him of being "hard kitsch". Ungers naturally got angry at that. He turned against Krier, who had taken the view that it was impossible to build as an architect under the prevailing conditions. Ungers found this unacceptable and explained that he had decided to return from the academic ivory tower and go back into practice, to "get his hands dirty" and get involved with the big developers.

If one wants to understand what Ungers does in his second creative phase, the attitude he expresses here is of decisive importance. So, as an artist, he says, "And now I'm producing the architecture you deserve." Of course, he doesn't write that anywhere, he can't, but I would say that this is the attitude behind it, behind all the coldness and hardness that Ungers' late work expresses so subliminally. But even if this is already conclusive in itself, I can still derive little from this attitude.

HK That actually goes back further. At the time when Ungers was realizing his early Cologne buildings, the role of technology in architecture was up for debate. During the symposium Ungers organized in Berlin in 1968, Reyner Banham summed it up by saying, "The architects will be surprised. If they don't get involved with technology, they'll disappear from the face of the earth."

At the eleventh CIAM Congress in Otterlo in 1959, there was a dispute between the Smithsons and Ernesto Nathan Rogers, which was basically a discussion about the London Roads Study on the one hand and the Torre Velasca on the other. The Italians had already decided where the journey would take them, but Ungers hadn't reached a conclusion yet. This was despite the fact that he, along with his early Cologne houses, including the one he built for himself, had already been identified by Aldo Rossi in 1960 as something exotic north of the Alps and had been presented as "un giovane architetto tedesco" in *Casabella Continuitá*. Ungers invited the Smithsons to the TU Berlin and published their *Without Rhetoric* in his series entitled *Publications on Architecture* as issue no. 2. There is something schizophrenic about this, coming after the legendary issue of *Wochenaufgaben 1964/65*, which miraculously anticipates his theme of architecture in breathtaking student drawings.

Only then came *Großformen im Wohnungsbau* as a first attempt at a morphological theory from Ungers, which called into question the functionalist blockade, including the one in people's heads.

Curiously, however, there then followed publications such as *Schnellstraße und Gebäude, Gutachten Ruhwald, Wohnsysteme in Stahl, Wohnsysteme in Großtafeln*, etc., which are characterized by an untroubled awareness of the progress of the time.

Into his American period, he tended towards this technocratic, not to say technicist side. The artistic then became more important to him, but he never opted for an architecture that accepted that there was an architectural history. He was not interested in the history of architecture in terms of convention and scale. He was only interested in the images from architectural history as raw material for the morphological pleasure of designing.

JC I don't think this is untypical. It's a modern attitude to deal with history only to overcome it and to come up with a supposed essence distilled from history—until, so to speak, only the trade secret remains. Then, of course, you quickly get to the idea that you can build the core form and omit the art form, and then you have this architecture from which everything has been sanded off.

HK From history, he was interested in the Renaissance tractates in their often mathematical rigorosity. Again, as a theory detached from practice. But history as a constructed tradition, which is basically critically continued by one's own work, is something he never made his own. This also made him very different from Colin Rowe, although they both agreed on many things.

JC Ungers has a certain essentialism, a search for the essence of architecture that is typically modern. This leads to the fact that you only want to build what is essential and omit everything else. And the essentials are body and space. If you take that to extremes, then you get the flat-ironed box. And that, I think, is the problem. But Ungers is, of course, in good keeping with his generation. There was a series of architects back then with completely different work, for example, Peter Eisenman, whose approach was nevertheless similar. It's just as Platonic. It's about realizing an idea.

HK I see it the same way. Every architect is placed in an era, and he or she deals with it more or less critically. In his time, Ungers saw and served the immense need to talk about architecture again. He undoubtedly brought German architecture back to the fore, at least on the architectural side.
They describe it as "leaving behind" Karlsruhe and Egon Eiermann, who could not talk much about architecture. Yet Eiermann was a brilliant design critic. He was a great entertainer and rigorously criticized design from the construction point of view. Ungers, on the other hand, felt a compulsion to talk about architecture again, not about construction or function, not about anything else that is part of a building. Eiermann began his lecture by recommending that you think carefully about whom you marry if you want to become an architect.

A little later, Ungers became concerned with art and architecture as art, even if one could be convinced that architecture was not only art but above all that it had to be useful in life. A condition he never accepted, not even in his own home, which he knew was so uncomfortable that one day he would be able to say that he and his wife Liselotte "live in this uncomfortable house." He did not say that it was a torture chamber, but he implicitly communicated that "we must live in it to maintain my idea of architecture, which I cannot betray." He doesn't go so far as to say that. But, basically, that's what's behind it.

JC That's why Ungers is more interesting with his ideas and values than with what he actually does. Because what he does is, of course, towards the end such a radical art form of life, which he can then only celebrate with himself. But that can no longer be generalized at all. You can't expect anyone to be put through that anymore. So, the house we are talking about here did not last half a year, and then it began to fall apart. He can only do that to himself. And in the end, it became very hermetic. You can see that from the fact that the house disappeared behind a thick hedge.

Remarkably, in the beginning, it was quite different. The first house he built is, from an ideological viewpoint, the complete opposite of his last. It is also a matter of concern to him to make himself understood by others.

There is a moment at the beginning of his career that fascinates me to this day, and that I would like to recall briefly. Ungers is in the process of making a name for himself and gets a real pasting. He is accused of being neo-expressionist in his architecture. What he designs is old hat. It's all been done before and done better. That's when he has to justify himself for the first time, and he gives a very important lecture, which he then develops further over a long period of time, and, in the end, it earns him his professorship in Berlin. Ungers compares four theatre buildings, namely by Aalto, Le Corbusier, Mies van der Rohe and Scharoun—that's not quite true: from Le Corbusier, he takes the parliament building in Chandigarh. And he says, "We have more or less the same programme here, and the same range of building technology is available—but they all look completely different, and now somebody explain it to me." But he's not saying that you can do what you want. His point is that the architect has to deal with the form because he or she is

Oswald Mathias Ungers
House without Qualities
Cologne 1995

not getting it from anywhere else. Otherwise, all designs would look the same. Ungers explains that the reason they are so different is that they are an expression of personal views. They show that there are different worlds of form that emerge from different ideologies.

Even though this may be a little too individualistic for us, what is decisive first and foremost is the insight that architecture cannot be explained by its conditions of production. Consequently, the architect not only has the freedom to determine the form, but this is also his responsibility.

And I still bring up this episode in my initial lectures to show that as an architect you have to have a position, that it's not about marketable recognition value, but about asking what you're actually there for as an architect. I think Ungers, especially the young Ungers, is extremely inspiring.

HK Absolutely! We share his assessment here and see all the more that in this regard it can't go any further. And why can't it? Because this generation was done with the history of architecture and wanted nothing more to do with it. One could have asked him to compare his oeuvre with that of Schinkel, Mies van der Rohe or Adolf Loos—architects whom he greatly appreciated. As an architect, I don't have the whole history of building behind me, but rather the dead architects who watch me at work and say, "What is this shit you're doing now?" Ungers was a charismatic speaker. I saw him at lectures in his debate with Colin Rowe. In Cornell, there were the Thursday evening lectures. One week Ungers spoke, the next week Rowe. That was incredible—a showdown! Ungers got so into it, he went home from those lectures soaked in sweat. The vehemence that was revealed there perhaps also had something to do with the repression of not letting history get to you. Colin Rowe was no different in his own way. For them, it was an existential confrontation, and for the students, it was an incredible lesson. I will never forget that.

JC I think there's only one way to go, and it's over at some point. I guess Ungers couldn't go any further. Is the understanding of history the problem? I think the problem is rather an exaggerated individualism, which is also very typical of this generation, which grew up with the Hitler Youth and then had to liberate itself and reinvent itself after the Second World War.

HK   Ernesto Rogers showed us how. In Otterlo, everyone, young and old, agreed that there was nothing left to be done with the concept of modernity. There was the position of the Smithsons and the Italians. The Torre Velasca is the key to getting involved in history and to envisaging a continuity of the city's regional architecture. That would be in line with Ungers, who constantly conjured up the genius loci.

JC   But maybe we are also bothered by something completely different—namely the Platonic "I don't care what it looks like" attitude. With Ungers, all of a sudden everything is somehow rasterized because the look isn't really important. Ungers is only interested in the disposition. Once that's clarified, the draft is ready. And it is only when one sees the designs side by side, and all the minimal nuances appear in the supposedly schematic that the whole becomes apparent. But, of course, that's so subtle and spiritual that you can't keep up with it as a normal mortal, and that's the real problem from my point of view.

HK   But this is also a generation problem. At this point, I would like to tell a story about Aldo Rossi, who appeared at the same time as the Smithsons at a symposium in Berlin. I was a student in my first semester. After Aldo Rossi had presented *The Architecture of the City*, he was rightly asked what all that had to do with his own architecture, the Gallaratese, for example. To which Aldo Rossi replied that his architectural language had nothing to do with that, but rather with the films he had seen and with his grandmother's dining table, on which coffee pots were placed and into which he always imagined himself going to see what kind of space was inside. From this, Rossi drew his architectural language. For him, that didn't have to go together with the theory of the city.

In the end, he took the step to become involved with urban development with his project on Schützenstraße in Berlin. Ungers was concerned with solitaires. He always resisted the corset of the parcel. Aldo Rossi gets involved in the urban development of the parcel and then builds this Berlin block with its colourful architecture as if from a child's construction kit. And because he is not satisfied with it, he comes along with the Palazzo Farnese and struggles, even if it is only a postmodern reference, to actually build this Michelangelo facade. This is the step that most contemporaries have not taken: to give the house an individual, tectonic physiognomy and not just a mask.

JC Now, one could also ask whether we are dealing here with a broad historical development—about which one could say that Ungers himself could only get as far as he could in his generation, and then it just continued in the generation after him where he left off—or with a special path that Ungers chooses in order to take a position at the end, from which it basically doesn't go any further. I think Ungers does the latter. He opted in favour of the idea and against the appearance. That is already very radical. In the end, he tries to show with the utmost rigour that it is—for the sake of failure!—about building ideas. And in this utter absurdity of actually knowing that this is not possible. In his last house, he pays no heed to climate or to construction technology—in short, to reality. That is a fundamental decision. Ungers plays a special role in his generation.

But from my point of view, the problem is, of course, the exaggerated individualism of this generation, in which everyone has to be an original genius in order to show that one hasn't been forced into line. Today, we are more prepared to say that architecture does not have to be reinvented every day. It has something to do with the city. It is about creating an environment that is pleasant for everyone. So, basically, we are back at the position of Adolf Loos—the house has to please everyone. Ungers' position is totally contrary. In a conversation, he once said that if you don't like my house, then go down another street.

HK In his early period in America, after the experiences of the first student riots in Berlin, he took up sociological and social topics in a rather naïve way and tried to build wooden houses with self-help groups. As an artist, as opposed to an architect, I can, of course, take the point of view that if they don't like it, then they just don't like it.

JC Up till now, perhaps, Ungers has come across as too much of a straightforward character. Of course, he is a person full of contradictions. There is also a lot of uncertainty in him. And out of this, he has also repeatedly appropriated the opinions of others, sometimes to such an extent that you are left flabbergasted. If, for example, you notice how much plagiarism there is in his texts.

There is a lot of attitude, but just as much opportunism. Or let's say he had great flexibility to get involved in things. This radicalism was the only way to stand firm, a protection from recurring self-doubt. And then comes this moment when he says that architecture is passé, we are now doing regional planning. He originally went to America with that in mind.

There are breaks and contradictions. Ungers often appears as someone who knows exactly what he wants, but there are always moments when his constructs collapse.

HK He had close contact with Rem Koolhaas when I was in America. Shortly before that, there was the competition project Welfare Island on which Rem worked. A week ago, Rem was interviewed about his Springer building in Berlin. He was asked how he would process the "today" in it. And that's when the keyword "reportage" came up. That interests Rem, he comes from film and scriptwriting and tries to grasp the phenomena of the time as a scenario, to sharpen them and make them pictorial. There he meets Ungers. For Ungers, the images were primarily a communication vehicle between him and his staff, the clients and the rest of the world, while Rem always feels challenged to make an architectural film.

Following this argument, I would accept his thoroughly post-modern preference, in which the two-dimensional image or the non-architectural product seems more important than the building itself. What is fascinating is that a project like the Märkisches Viertel can function as an image, as an idea, and even as a sociological arrangement in the floor plan of an apartment. It is a wonderfully archaic idea that the apartment, the house and, in the end, the city can be derived from the family. This works on many levels and has something Roman about it. But if you stand in front of the twenty-storey towers, the ground floor looks exactly like the top floor, there is no roof, then reality is shattering in its dreariness—two square meters of doorbells, nobody cares about the house. All this has been excluded.

JC This is actually one of the biggest blind spots in Ungers' thinking. It fascinates me in many aspects but also shocks me in others. It's a lack of magnitude. It makes no difference how big or small something is. The ideas, or even the pictures, are arbitrarily scalable with him, and, of course, it becomes unarchitectural. There is no scale.

HK There is something tragic about this. He collects count-less treatises and takes from them the image of the Vitruvian Man, but he only deals with it geometrically and mathemati-cally and turns it into the shape of the square and the grid. As an anthropomorphic component, which in turn has something to do with proportion, or, in other words, with an understanding of proportion that is not found abstractly in geometry but has to do with one's physical sensation in relation to the artifact, he does not allow it to touch him, although he has read Wölfflin and Schmarsow.

JC Yes, the whole haptic is basically missing.

HK I would be even harsher. It is a misunderstanding of proportion. For me, proportion only has something to do with geometry at the edge. Proportion is the relationship between artifact and man. Man perceives his counterpart and establish-es a relationship.

JC I think the last house Ungers built for himself, which is very clearly proportioned, is the best example of this misunder-standing. It's a vicious circle: if you start to reduce everything further and further to pure proportion, then you can only do less and less, and in the end, it seems like a faux pas if there's only one ordinary fizzy water bottle on the table. It won't fit in there anymore. That's what you get from this kind of escalation.

HK If we make a clean break here and review the era of the 1960s, when Ungers built his first houses and also took his first steps in teaching, then we are in an age without architectural discourse.
There was functionalism, and that was it. I can remember com-petition juries, some time later, where there were drawings of huge residential project views—facade was not said, there could be no facades—on a scale of 1:500. At a jury meeting with Max Bächer, I pointed out that facades had to be drawn at least on a scale of 1:100 in order to be able to talk about the quality of the designs at all. They fobbed me off with: "As architects, we obviously know that, but we can imagine it on this scale." Stupidity without equal.
You had to go abroad. So I came to Vienna to study with Hans Hollein. He couldn't talk about architecture either, but he had

an opulent formal repertoire that functionalism completely lacked. It was only in America that I was confronted with the entire pre-war tradition of art history and architectural theory. There, I also noticed that teachers like Colin Rowe, who was influenced by the Warburg Institute in London, and especially by Wittkower, drew from this. And this was much earlier than Ungers. At that time, I sat in the library with Thomas Will day and night to catch up on all the things we had been denied in Germany. When I was a student in Germany, I didn't know Wölfflin or Schmarsow or Sitte or Stübben. I didn't know anything about this at all. Of course, there was a library in Karlsruhe, but that was for studying the history of art and architecture, which had nothing to do with the theory of design.

JC   In Ungers' defence, it has to be said that he at least surrounded himself with history. How he did this is shown very impressively when you look at his library. First, there is this white scaffolding and then there are the books. I can understand that in relation to the overall spatial impression because you don't want to be bowled over by the books. But that also says something. First, there is your own conceived idea, and then there are the books behind it. They are almost a kind of wallpaper. There are also plenty of things he couldn't even read, for example all those Italian treatises. So, there is also a little bit of information there. But, along with the need for a certain aura, I think it is also a sense for the wealth of experience of history that shows itself here. And Ungers started collecting treatises and things like that early on. He was quite unique in this at the end of the 1950s.

HK   Nobody was interested. Nobody was interested in history. Not even expressionism. When we started building in Holland and mentioned the Amsterdam School, everyone threw their hands up in the air, even in Holland!
There was one big exception: Otto Ernst Schweizer. He taught building typology in Karlsruhe, but he was also a building architect. He built a remarkable stadium in Nuremberg—modern architecture of the interwar period. He gave this blatantly anachronistic building typology lesson. I have often asked Ungers, who studied with him, about it. He never really reacted to it. There have been publications by Otto Ernst Schweizer in which he deals with historical building typologies and city

Oswald Mathias Ungers
House Ungers
Cologne 1990

plans. They go back a long way to the Renaissance, Rome and Greece. In addition, there were uncompromisingly modern designs that seemed schizophrenic to me because the link was broken and a connection could not be seen even with the best will in the world.

There was architecture and art history. That really interested me, but it had absolutely nothing to do with what I was involved in as a prospective architect. I couldn't make that connection at the time. If I flip through my notes today, I learn that, like an autodidact, I have acquired this tradition in the meantime through the practice of designing and building.

JC   I believe that within Ungers lies an unspoken, ultimately Hegelian understanding of historicity. It is basically the idea that once you have understood the whole logic, you don't really need history anymore. He tries to penetrate to the essential and to knock down everything insignificant. Otto Ernst Schweizer also does this in a certain way.

And, of course, this raises the question of how rational that actually is, and whether it is even possible to name the essence of something unambiguously. In my opinion, this is where the fundamental error lies. One thinks one can say what is important—but one quickly miscalculates and, in any case, one just reduces everything—and then one no longer deals with the phenomena themselves. If you did that, you would continue to be part of history and remain connected to it, precisely by trying to understand houses as houses and not as an expression of ideas that you think you have finally found. And then you stop searching. That's the problem.

HK   It is also due to abstraction. This form of historicity can only be approached as abstraction, but not as a concrete phenomenon with which one has to deal intellectually, possibly even physically.

JC   But perhaps we have simply reached the limit of what Ungers and his generation were able to work on in terms of content. He was able to bring architecture back to itself a good deal anyway.

And in order to come back to what we can learn from Ungers, I would like to emphasize an aspect that is also of great importance in his teaching, namely the confrontation with reality—

his willingness to face the facts. That is also the reason why Koolhaas came to him at that time. And there is still a lot in it today. I would just like to remind you of the debate about Berlin as a city and the question of how to fully utilize and reinforce transport infrastructures and other factors. His teaching in Berlin is dedicated to this question, and it always revolves around seeing how an idea would affect reality. I am thinking specifically about the Berlin 1995 project, in which the idea of "megastructure" and the reality of "Berlin" literally crash into each other in order to produce new insights. That was really very fruitful.

And you also have to ask who dealt with the urban in a comparable way in the 1960s. There was hardly anyone who did anything clever, and here it is something special: Ungers' return to the city and to the question of how architecture and the city belong together and how the city can also be made through architecture.

HK   Basically, yes. But above all, the confrontation with Colin Rowe brought me back to a lasting understanding of the city. Ungers was about an abstract concept of the city. The Braunschweig Study, in which I was involved, could be mentioned here as an example. The aim was not to gain an analytical understanding of the urban situation, but rather to first discuss what is actually there. It was about a series of trees, about a wall of houses, about the street itself. These things were typologically singled out and documented as starting material for the morphological transformation of the respective urban situation. But it wasn't about the urban space or street space, nor about the facades.

In his own work—and Ungers realized many projects in urban situations—this was not an issue because he thought too conceptually or from a bird's-eye perspective and was focused on solitary architectures. He did not go through these designs in his mind.

He created few situations in which an urban space is formed, with the exception of the Galleria of the Frankfurt Fair. This is a typological element that becomes spatially effective. Otherwise, it is actually always solitaires that could occasionally, should other solitaires join them, become an urban space.

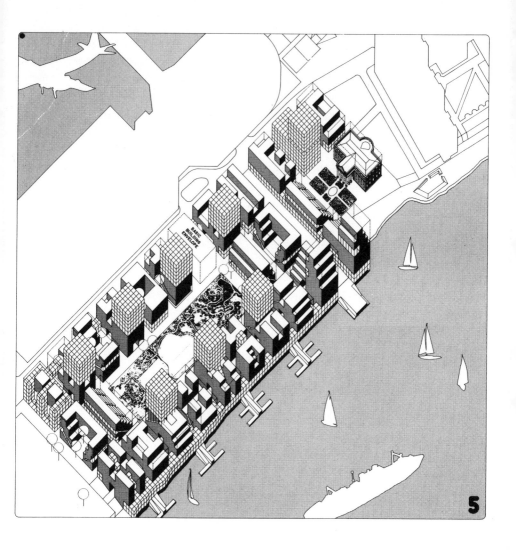

Oswald Mathias Ungers
Competition entry Roosevelt Island Housing
New York 1975

JC I would say that these are opportunities that are lost in the realization. The buildings only become solitaires because they look so "Ungers-like" and thus stand out. When I look at the competition designs that Ungers returned with in the second half of the 1970s, I often find that his designs won the day because they cut the best figure in terms of urban planning compared to the other submitted works. The fact that the realization is so schematic is the real problem. One could say that Ungers was getting better and better as an urban planner and worse and worse as an architect.

HK I think these urban development projects are rather isolated, projects like the Grünzug Süd in Cologne and Lichterfelde 4. Ring in Berlin no longer existed in his later oeuvre. Lichterfelde is a project conceived in a very spatial way, although nowhere was a perspective shown that reveals the cubature and the volumetric relationship of the urban building blocks.

JC There are plenty of axonometries for that.

HK Yes, but they show everything only from above. Ungers always thought from a bird's-eye view. Even with the Welfare Island project, where it would have been appropriate to go into the street and to give at least an idea of the scale.
The exception is the competition entry for the Wallraf-Richartz-Museum in Cologne. A perspective was drawn from this, the one with the Magritte man. I don't know any others.
Everything is thought about from the top view. That is an accusation one has to make against him. This is also the case in the projects that were created later in Berlin. For example, the design for Humboldthafen, in which the square became the ultimate tool for getting to grips with the most contradictory of things.
To be honest, simply putting a square frame around Humboldthafen, with this brutal crossing of the railway lines, their clumsy substructure and all of it above the most fragile and wonderful urbanistic outline in Berlin, which we owe to Lenné, is at best a careless or even a cynical commentary on these hopeless conditions.

JC I agree. This morphological method, this idea of an encyclopedic city, ends up dead.

HK If the early Ungers had gone there, or the Ungers of the Lichterfelde project, he would have discovered and developed an immense repertoire of urban and architectural possibilities.

On the other hand, there was a project on Schillerstraße in which he really pulled out all the morphological stops and was lastingly surprised, struck and injured by reality. I didn't work on the project, but I remember how depressed he was when he came back from Berlin. He hadn't drawn the windows yet, and they were ready on the construction site. That was the devastating reality that still exists today. Nevertheless, many architects come to terms with it. I haven't done that for a long time. After this experience, he could have said, now it's over, if you've already bought the windows, you can do the rest on your own. But he clung to it. It was his first project in Berlin and his foot in the door, so to speak.

It's really a catastrophically bad project, not only because the windows were bought without agreement and because the craftsmanship is completely substandard, but also because the morphological logic led to unacceptable spatial conflicts. How one lives in it, how one's design fits into the street when two houses further on are still beautiful buildings from the *Gründerzeit*, did not interest him. He was not even interested in the fact that the corner of the house made a mockery of its constructivist role model.

JC But Ungers soon noticed that this approach didn't work. So he changed his course and left all poetic attempts behind.

HK For me, however, all this is still extremely important today. It is an instrument that in no way imposes architecture that is to be dreaded. You can use it to design and build great things. If we're really interested in architecture, there's no other way. These "poetic attempts" point beyond the mere construction.

JC That brings us back to the beginning. Ungers is the great teacher.

HK Absolutely! To put it in a nutshell: the rationalists, Manfredo Tafuri or Jonas Geist, whom I experienced at the Hochschule der Künste Berlin, spoke of chaos and showed pictures of destruction in which everything was blown apart because the circumstances allegedly did not allow anything better. This was roughly based on the slogan that there could be no good life in the bad. Scenarios like in the final scene of the film *Zabriskie Point*.

But how do you deal with that, even if you accept it as a hypothesis? In Germany it was no hypothesis; in Germany the destruction was real. There were seas of debris, especially intellectual debris. In this atmosphere, it was impossible to simply restore the destroyed streets. You couldn't even hope for that.

The modernist option was to deal with the situation with utopian concepts. The Smithsons, with the walkways on the first floor and the traffic flowing underneath, or the giant buildings of Scharoun, stretched from Charlottenburg to Kreuzberg, or the ideas of Le Corbusier, who was probably the most sensible. The other possibility, and this was something in which Ungers was interested, was to discover an aesthetic appeal in what was already there. Ungers' inability to restore the old, neither mentally nor from his material possibilities, offered him the chance to face the situation and make the best of it. Basically, his aim was to accept the chaos of the big picture, to cling to certain fragments on a small scale and to create a new poetic architecture out of them that was useful, perhaps durable and possibly even beautiful.

That was a way of dealing with history that I, too, could relate to. Many projects were created on the periphery during this time in West Berlin. For us back then, the periphery was the place of promise. One was inspired to develop something new and fascinating out of the fragments. He provided the intellectual potential and the language for that. That's Ungers.

Hans Kollhoff studied architecture in Karlsruhe and Vienna. After receiving his diploma in 1975, he became the assistant of O. M. Ungers at Cornell University. Since 1978 he has run an architecture office in Berlin, initially with Arthur Ovaska, and since 1984 with Helga Timmermann. Alongside his work as an architect, Kollhoff has been teaching architecture since the 1980s. After visiting professorships at the HdK Berlin and the University of Dortmund, he was Professor for Architecture and Design at ETH Zurich from 1990 to 2012. He frequently publishes texts and essays in daily newspapers, magazines and books. Among his works are the Piraeus housing block in Amsterdam, completed in 1994, the DaimlerChrysler Skyscraper in Berlin, finished in 2000, and the Ministry of the Interior and Ministry of Justice in The Hague, completed in 2013.

Jasper Cepl, born in 1973, is Professor for Architectural Theory at the Hochschule Anhalt in Dessau. After studying at RWTH Aachen and the Technical University of Berlin, he received his doctoral and postdoctoral qualification at the TU Berlin. He is the author of various publications including *Oswald Mathias Ungers. Eine intellektuelle Biographie*, the edited monograph *Hans Kollhoff: Kollhoff & Timmermann Architects* and the anthology *Quellentexte zur Architekturtheorie* with Fritz Neumeyer.

Oswald Mathias Ungers was born in Kaisersesch in 1926 and died in Cologne in 2007. From 1947 to 1950, he studied architecture at the Technical University of Karlsruhe. In addition to founding his architectural practice in Cologne and later in Berlin, Frankfurt am Main and Karlsruhe, he was a professor at the Technical University of Berlin, Cornell University in Ithaca, Harvard University in Cambridge, the University of California in Los Angeles, the University of Applied Arts in Vienna and the Art Academy in Düsseldorf. His numerous buildings include the Deutsches Architekturmuseum in Frankfurt am Main, 1984, the House without Qualities in Cologne, 1995, and the Wallraf-Richartz-Museum in Cologne, 2001.

on Ludwig Mies van der Rohe

with Monika Sosnowska

The conversation between Monika Sosnowska and Tom Emerson on Mies van der Rohe, in contrast to the mostly uniform review, reflects a particular and distinctly personal confrontation with the great name Mies van der Rohe.

MS Ludwig Mies van der Rohe—where do we start with such a big subject?

TE I don't know your work encyclopedically, but I saw your show more than ten years before we met. That was the first time that your work became quite visible in the UK. I have seen it published here and there since. And, of course, your work called *Tower* is a research project based on Mies van der Rohe. How did you get from Poland to Chicago?

MS At the beginning of preparing my projects, I was not really interested in Mies van der Rohe or in architecture in general. Rather, I was observing the city and its changes. I moved to Warsaw from Amsterdam in 2000, and Warsaw was undergoing a big transformation from communism to capitalism, which was very visible in the city. I started observing the things happening around me. I was looking at my neighbourhood, at housing estates and office buildings, things from mass production, almost like no-name architecture. I did several projects based on this, and a couple of years later I started travelling more within Europe and also to other continents. I decided to check where modernism came from. I visited the Bauhaus in Dessau, the Rietveld buildings in Amsterdam, some buildings of Le Corbusier, and Mies happened also on the way. I saw his Barcelona Pavilion, the Tugendhat house in Brno and then I travelled to Chicago. Obviously, in Chicago, Mies was the most visible architect. Later, I had the opportunity to do a bigger project in New York, and I decided to pick Mies. It was a fragment of the curtain wall facade from the Lake Shore Drive Apartments, but I treated it in a brutal way. I took it and bent it as a newspaper so it became a horizontally lying collapsed tower. I think Mies seemed to be an ideal example of modernism, almost like a matrix for the kind of second-hand version of modernism that I had observed before in Poland. I also had the chance to look at Mies's works a little more carefully. But I am not an architect, so I look at the buildings as an average person. That's probably why I took the facade and not the construction of the building. I look at the houses as they appear in the city.

TE And when you started looking at Mies, could you actually feel the connection back to your experience in Warsaw,

Ludwig Mies van der Rohe
Lake Shore Drive Apartments
Chicago 1951

and Polish modernism when you saw the American architecture from the 1950s?

> MS   Yes, although the version in Poland has a more human touch, I would say. It's not that perfect in proportions or in craft. Modernism in Poland in the 1960s happened at a time when the economy collapsed, so there was a lack of materials and budgets. Modernism was not executed well, whereas Mies in America—even after so many years—is a perfect and ideal example. But I took the idea of his building and produced it in Poland. So, I gave it a human touch again. I worked with my fabricators, who are welders rather than art craftsmen. I took Mies back to Poland and made him a more second-hand version again.

TE   I associate your work predominantly with steel. Is there something about steel as a material for making things, outside of its architectural, political or historical contexts, that you have a particular interest or fascination with?

> MS   I am not particularly interested in steel or in any other material. I'm interested more in the subject. So, the connection of being interested in architecture from the 1960s and Mies van der Rohe is kind of clear. Especially the curtain wall facade, which I understood as a manifestation of modernism. But it also comes from my different perspective and approach towards architecture. I see it the other way around to architects because they start from the structure and then they cover the building. I have observed the process the other way around. So, for me, steel represents the bones, the essence of the buildings.

TE   I think there is something about steel that suits your process. Steel is a very direct expression of modernism. Essentially, steel bends, and when you bend steel hard enough, it stays like that, and it bears all the physical, spatial traces of the forces you have applied to it, the distortions.

> MS   Yes, maybe you're right, but it also fits the idea I would like to express. I think I am at the other end of Mies, because my works are about failure, about the end of something. Mies was very optimistic when he was building a new world, a new order.

Monika Sosnowska
Tower
2014

Monika Sosnowska
Tower
2014

TE That is interesting because, in my opinion, Mies is very ambivalent about the future. He is very mysterious because he pretends to be rational but, actually, he is more mystical. He wanted to represent the world as he saw it. He doesn't declare a political or social project with it.

MS OK, but he was inventing a new language. Those shapes did not exist before.

TE Of course, he was unbelievably inventive. But I think his motivation was inventing the now, not inventing the future, which is politically quite a different project.

MS Do you think he had no ambitions to build the entire world, to change the entire world?

TE No, I don't think he wanted to change the world. He wanted to record it in some way.

MS Maybe he was thinking of creating a measuring tape, something that everyone can refer to. This could be the point at which to ask why you are interested in Mies van der Rohe?

TE I had never thought about it in those terms. But I like the idea that he is a measure of a certain moment, of a certain culture, a certain society in flux.

MS But you seem quite different to him, as a person and as an architect as well.

TE Yes, completely. But perhaps I am drawn to him because he authored part of his mythology, and then lots of people followed. And I think that a lot of the Mies that you read about has been very neatly framed by certain rhetorical and historical positions including rationalism. I think he is an incurable romantic.

MS Aha!

TE His work is not really rational. It is extremely beautiful, and it gets quite close to being rational, technical and innovative. It is interesting that the facades he did in Chicago failed technically. People had buckets in their apartments, and they were overheating. All this was built before air conditioning. Those buildings were like glasshouses. Or the buildings that he did in IIT with these amazing brick bases. He does a 130-metre brick wall with no movement joint, and then he puts the biggest piece of glass that could be produced on top of it. The whole thing cracked. I find it amazing that he never got sacked from IIT.

MS But he had to experiment.

TE And he had an institutional client who would allow him to experiment and fail, which is testament to his incredible charisma. Even at the age of 25, he would be at some society soirée in Aachen, and then he would just walk up to the main person and say, "I'll design a house for you." He had unbelievable confidence. He could bring people along with him on these experiments.

MS So, is he more metaphorical than technical?

TE I think that he likes the idea of structure more than in the most optimized technical, economic solution. He wants the idea to be perfect, and in that sense, he often makes use of structure in a quite metaphorical sense. For example, the Barcelona Pavilion has these skinny columns taking down the load. And then there are these massive onyx walls going through it. If anything was ever made to take load, then it is stone not pins. I think he placed the stone to create a landscape, not a structure. Or in Lakeshore Drive, he talks about five reasons why those elements are on the facade: one is to keep the facade stiff, one of them is to optimize the size of the window and so on. All of them are good pragmatic reasons, but then he goes on with the fifth one: because it looks good. On the corner, there is an extra one that is technically not required. He is technically very sophisticated, but I don't think he has an ethical alliance with a direct kind of truthfulness about things.

MS I even think that he was more an artist than an architect. That his works are kind of finished. While architecture for me is very much determined by many things like clients, politics and

Ludwig Mies van der Rohe
German Pavilion
Barcelona 1929

places, he seems to manage to go over all that. He is somehow working for the epoch.

TE Yes, he managed to contain it in something bigger, and his ambition is quite incredible. He uses the word "epoch" over and over. It has something epic about it and sounds like it has something to do with civilisation.

MS Exactly. How can you think on such a scale? It is incredible. Especially in the times he was working in.

TE I also think he hit America at a moment when it was ready for him and he was ready for it. That was an incredible and very beautiful coincidence. That, to some extent, gave almost full expression to the twentieth century. In a way, it is comparable to Le Corbusier, whose work became increasingly personal and spiritual, whereas Mies was getting increasingly universal. Just think about the number of copies and how it became a model. His work and his ideas have produced so many different imitators, some of them brilliant, like mid-century SOM, the early Smithsons, Eames and, I would also argue, Gehry—but that is maybe more controversial—and lots of more anonymous examples. Cities throughout the world are full of versions of Mies. Some of them are incredibly beautiful, completely anonymous, but you come around the corner and suddenly there is this very ordinary bit of city that has a kind of dignity that is one, two steps above being functional. And his legacy is really interesting because it also has caused a few monsters like that corporate vernacular that just marches across cities. One of his nicer quotes is from when he was interviewed and asked how he felt about the fact that Philip Johnson was taking credit for the Seagram Building: "Oh, that's OK, just as long as he doesn't give me credit for some of his buildings."

MS It would be interesting to hear more about your approach to Mies. Your work doesn't usually speak the structural language of Mies's work. But at the moment, you are working on the steel construction for the MK Gallery. What did you take or learn from Mies?

TE I'm interested in the way Mies made a meta-project of modernity. The way that he went from European modernism, which combined certain traditions and crafts with abstraction, to America where he developed a very different type of modernism. He, more than anyone else, made his early European work in a context in which it's almost impossible to be modern. And then in America, there is a profound transformation in his work. Suddenly he finds a space where he can only be modern but where there is no language for it yet. The early tall buildings of Chicago are steel-framed, but they are still dressed in old European clothes like oversized palazzi. But he is the one who makes a new image of the American city that goes right the way through from his selection of I-sections on the facade to a register of the whole American landscape. So, he managed to get to this unbelievable complexity and find a way of articulating it in very simple means. He did that with steel, he did that with spatial structures, he did that even with the idea of social space. He had a quite strong sense of what society is, even if he was quite silent on ideological and political declarations. And I am interested in his relationship to nature. The moment he drew the glass tower for the competition in Friedrichstraße in black charcoal, he knew that nature is everywhere, especially in glass, which is an optical mystery. Those drawings were published everywhere but still, for the rest of the century, people pretended that glass was transparent. I don't look at Mies formally. But he has a way of thinking about the relationship between the rational and the irrational that I really find fascinating. There is a logic to things, but in the end, the premise has a bigger aim, which is more ambiguous and more mysterious.

MS Could you live in a house designed by Mies?

TE There is a really beautiful small house that he made just outside Berlin. Just the last one he did before he went to America. It is very, very beautiful. Also, the Krefeld villas of his early period seem like they are amazing to live in. I could easily have the Farnsworth House as my weekend house, or I could spend a couple of nights in the Barcelona Pavilion. It would be interesting because that's almost not a building, that's Mies as the landscape architect. But I couldn't live in the Tugendhat house. I've been there a couple of times. It's amazing but it's a palace.

MS There is a sentence from Oskar Hansen when people were complaining about his housing block, that it's all wrong and they don't feel comfortable: "No, the architecture is right, people failed."

TE It is often the case with the more visionary things.

MS Mies was also a stonemason's son. Did this handicraft background play a role in the directness of his architecture?

TE Yes, I think that this is quite deep in it. Not only that he was a stonemason's son, but his brother was the stonecutter, and he was the typographer. He cut the letters in it, and then his sister did the gold leafing. It was a nice family business. I've seen pictures of some of the gravestones in Aachen. You can see in the typography that he has an incredibly elegant mind.

Tom Emerson was born in Paris, France in 1970 and studied architecture at the University of Bath, the Royal College of Art and the University of Cambridge. In 2001, together with Stephanie Macdonald, he founded 6a architects in London. He taught at the Architectural Association in London from 2000 to 2004, at the University of Cambridge from 2004 to 2010 and has been a professor at the ETH in Zurich since 2010. During the course of his teaching and research activities, he constructed the Pavilion of Reflections on Lake Zurich for Manifesta 11, and his studies on urban landscapes in Forst, Galway and Glasgow were exhibited at the Glasgow International Biennale. He has produced several publications and articles, including *Never Modern*, 2013, and *My Bauhaus*, 2018. His built works include the Cowan Court in Cambridge, 2017, and the MK Gallery in Milton Keynes, 2019.

Monika Sosnowska was born in Ryki, Poland in 1972 and studied at the Academy of Fine Arts in Poznan. Subsequently, she completed a postgraduate course at the Rijksakademie van Beeldende Kunsten in Amsterdam. In her large-format installations, she deals with the deformation of structural architectural components, including the facade constructions of Mies van der Rohe. In 2003 she received the prestigious Baloise Art Prize in Basel and the Polityka's Passport award in Poland. Her work has appeared in numerous international solo and group exhibitions, including *Projects 83: Monika Sosnowska*, Museum of Modern Art, New York, 2006, *Monika Sosnowska, Andrea Zittel 1:1*, Schaulager, Basel, 2008, and *Living Cities*, Tate Modern, London, 2017. In 2007 she represented Poland at the 52nd Venice Biennale.

Ludwig Mies van der Rohe was born in Aachen in 1886 and died in Chicago in 1969. After an apprenticeship as a bricklayer, he worked with Bruno Paul and later with Peter Behrens in Berlin. At the same time, he worked on his own initial projects. After World War I, he attracted attention with his visionary contribution to the Friedrichstraße competition in 1921. His important early works include his residential building in the Weißenhofsiedlung Stuttgart in 1927, the Barcelona Pavilion in 1929 and the Villa Tugendhat in Brno in 1930. In 1930 he was appointed director of the Bauhaus, which he led until 1933. In 1938 he moved to the USA and founded his own architectural office in Chicago, while at the same time teaching at the Armour Institute (later called the Illinois Institute of Technology). Among his late works are the Farnsworth House, 1951, the Lake Shore Drive Apartments, 1951, the campus of the IIT along with the Crown Hall, 1956, the Seagram Building in New York, 1958, and the New National Gallery in Berlin, 1967.

Mario Botta

on Louis I. Kahn

with
Pippo Ciorra

The conversation between Mario Botta and
Pippo Ciorra on Louis I. Kahn links Botta's
personal history and his own work with Kahn's
work. It reflects on his first encounter with
Kahn, draws parallels and comparisons with
Carlo Scarpa and provides insights into fundamental theses of academic teaching.

MB Talking about Louis Kahn means talking about architecture and the problems of our days. He has been somewhat forgotten over the past decades to make way for postmodernism and projects with more spectacular forms, but I think it is more important today than ever to learn from such a profound personality. Kahn got to the bottom of problems and is an architect of great relevance in the face of globalization, the multitude of cultures and consumption.

PC In my many years of dealing with Kahn, I discovered several facets of his work and his person for myself.
Initially, it was the American, vernacular architect Kahn who was able to practice architecture in an almost mystical way, creating architecture of spaces, light and material, made accessible to us by our teachers because he was supposed to have learned from the lesson of Rome's archaeology.
Later, following some of my PhD students' research work, I found myself dealing with his organic, modular structures, his exploration of the spatiality of rooms and their multiplication, the Kahn of the 1950s.
Finally, there is a Louis Kahn that we are only beginning to see now: Kahn, in his historical context, a way of looking at him that reveals his true value.
Mario, how was it for you? You met him personally very early on, didn't you?

MB I met him, together with the historian Giuseppe Mazzariol, during my studies in 1968 on the occasion of his design for the Palazzo dei Congressi in Venice. At the time, a local team was sought to assist him with this project.
I remember that he was sending us interesting questions in the form of telegrams in which, for example, he asked for the dimensions of the existing trees on the building site. So we went to the Giardini, where the Biennale is located, measured up the trees and sent him the drawings. He asked for more information by return—he needed the girth of the trees. So I measured it and sent it to him again.
He was looking for a biological and an anthropological understanding of the place to decode people's behaviour and feelings in the specific situation.
This is the Louis Kahn I have come to know. A Louis Kahn who, before he started the project, wanted to understand what

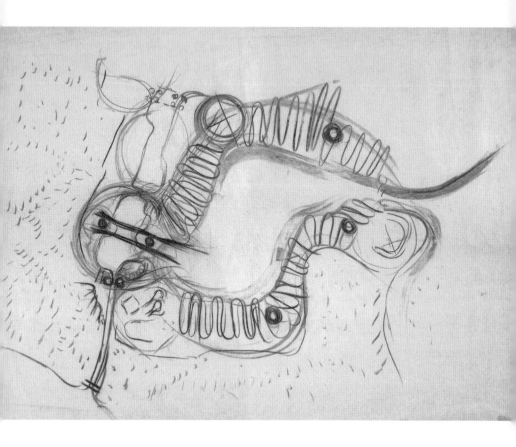

Louis I. Kahn
Palazzo dei Congressi
Venice 1968–1974

Louis I. Kahn
Palazzo dei Congressi
Venice 1968–1974

determined the reality of the context. During the development of the Palazzo dei Congressi, Kahn had two intuitions that still impress me. On the one hand, he interpreted the project, in contrast to comparable designs of the time, not as an anonymous space, but as an agora, as a place of encounter and discussion. This is still an appropriate point of view today. He was a prophetic man. I met the prophet Louis Kahn.

Another aspect of this page of Kahn, which I got to know as a student, is the following anecdote. During a discussion in which we asked the maestro what school was for him, he replied that school for him is two people talking under a tree. He spoke of the idea of communication and of being protected. Kahn spoke from his prophetic point of view about the essence. He had the ability to get to the bottom of problems, the ability to abstract phenomena into a schema, themes that you have also addressed, the idea of the vernacular by Vincent Joseph Scully, the modular system, the theme of light or the theme of gravity.

I am still surprised that he later returned to America and fell into oblivion. He disappeared to make way for postmodernism. Michael Graves, Stanley Tigerman and their fellows took over the discourse. They served the longing of the time for a visual language of memory. Personally, I think postmodernism styles were confused with history. The desire for history and memory was real, but many architects simplified it into a citation of isolated elements—a pillar, a gable. Kahn went on to the origins of the problems. For him, history was a constant companion on the journey of an architect.

My encounters as a young student in Venice with Carlo Scarpa and Kahn changed my life. In my opinion, architecture would not have been possible without them. I later discovered the fundamental idea of gravity through Kahn. Our generation had experienced a total distortion of architectural values. One spoke exclusively about lightness, which was fixed as a fact of architecture.

But in contrast to this point of view, the architectural facts actually get their meaningfulness from gravity, not from lightness.

If it is lightness that presupposes the creation of an aeroplane, I understand that. But if you design a building that is connected to the earth, it is about something fundamentally different.

PC It is rather something that belongs in the world of the fantastic, in nowhere places like in Italo Calvino's stories.

MB Right. In this respect, Kahn is also the one who pointed out the limits of technological development. He had nothing against technology per se, he was enthusiastic about it, but he understood it in the sense of an instrument to offer people added value. He criticized the consumption established by technology and revealed how it became multiplied in the society of consumption. With this position, he is the last master of the modern movement. The masters who preceded him are the Post-Bauhaus icons, Le Corbusier, Mies, Gropius and Scharoun.

PC I would like to highlight another facet of Kahn's work. To my knowledge, Kahn was the one who brought archaeology into the architectural debate and re-established an awareness of history there through the acknowledgement of the archaeological lesson.
This can also be seen in his understanding of the wall, which was never merely interpreted as a sign, but as a space-creating element, and perhaps that is something that can also be found in the architecture of Mario Botta. In your work, you often refer to the triangle—Scarpa, Le Corbusier and Kahn. As a superficial observer looking at your work, I recognize Scarpa and Kahn more clearly than, for example, Le Corbusier. So, the question is, did Kahn help you leave Le Corbusier behind?

MB These three masters you have mentioned are formative figures of our generation. It is not possible to leave Le Corbusier behind. Le Corbusier's strength was that he transformed events of daily life into architecture. In the years between the two World Wars, there existed the idea of the *Existenzminimum*. During this period, Le Corbusier invented the Ville Radieuse as a model of collective living. In response to the need for a new piety, he developed the monastery La Tourette and the church in Ronchamp. Le Corbusier is a man who changed the history of the twentieth century through architecture. Before him, at the beginning of the century, eclectic architecture prevailed, an architecture that responded to the conditions of various functions, but without having a language of its own.

Le Corbusier transformed the events of contemporary history into a contemporary language of architecture. For this reason alone, it is not possible to leave Le Corbusier behind.

> PC   In your opinion, Le Corbusier hit the zeitgeist. But is that something you would deny to Louis Kahn?

MB   Kahn worked differently. In my opinion, Kahn is a critical personality in architecture. When he pointed out the lost value of the wall with his theses, he also asked indirectly, what have you been doing since the beginning of the century?
He developed his argument as follows: the walls at the beginning of the century were thick stone walls that defined the space of the city and the space of man; with the industrial spread of brick, which also had a higher insulating capacity, they became thinner; then building with reinforced concrete was established; then the curtain wall, made of glass, was developed and finally the wall became a puff of air that—even today—separates the interior from the exterior.
He not only denounced the loss of gravity, of weight, thus of space and thus of architectural value represented in this development, but also showed how architecture was deprived of the ability to compensate for heat and cold and how a dependence on fossil energy was created. Kahn himself had nothing against air conditioning, but he pleaded for good construction and a series of mediations to create a link between inside and outside. It boils down to the fact that what inspires and amazes me about architecture is created in relation to the conditions of space and not in relation to the conditions of technology, of functional solutions.
Kahn is of great topicality at a time when the meaningfulness of architectural forms is dissolving. Let us take only the international dissemination of certain modes of construction. I am currently working in China, India and Korea, and it hurts me to see how the same construction model of glass and cement and the same understanding of interior and exterior prevail in all places. This no longer has anything to do with what the masters understood from architecture when they talked about the relationship, the symbiosis with the climate, when they pointed out that architecture belongs to the culture of the territory.

PC   Another of Kahn's major creative areas is his work on town planning. Do you agree with me that there are some contradictions here between Kahn as the draftsman of the city and the architect Kahn, who often created solitaires?

MB   Kahn was confronted with problems that are still prevalent today. His examination of the city itself led to the realization that a city built from scratch would not work.
There were the models Chandigarh by Le Corbusier or Brasilia by Lúcio Costa, which, however, were not developed from the point of view of a functional optimization from which Kahn operated. His contribution was to direct the architectural discourse towards the theme of territory. In addition, Kahn was able to create building dimensions with a human scale by multiplying cell units and also to give these new structures a city crown by adding them together.
From a historical perspective, this example makes clear how important Kahn's lessons are, and that they can be understood in some way as a critique of the modernity of the 1950s.

PC   When one thinks of his religious buildings, it is noticeable that the theme of the human scale that you have mentioned plays a major role. Kahn develops spatial proportions with extraordinary sensitivity. Is that something you could learn from him?

MB   I don't want to start defending my work, but I learned a lot from Kahn. I hope at least intellectually. Recently I curated the exhibition *Spazio Sacro* in Locarno, where twenty-two places of cult were shown—twenty-two works that endure in a secularized world, even if today people are seen less frequently in church. On display are built works, synagogues, mosques and churches, forms of religious expression and spiritual values, which at the same time satisfy a certain desire for memory. I deeply agree with Kahn when he says that the past is a friend. For Kahn, the past is always part of the present. Today, modern culture is about displacing the past. You discard the old to have the new that doesn't even last a season. Kahn also developed profound thoughts in this respect. With the event of the moon landing, he saw a time coming in which the necessity of a great past became inevitable. In this context, Kahn reminds us of the still valid values of gravity, light and material.

For me, his work and his teaching are of great critical topicality. Here, I am less interested in a direct confrontation with the images of what he has built. In my opinion, it is not essential to deal with Kahn's formal language, which can be somewhat exaggerated in the contrast of volumes or light moods. However, his ideas, theses and themes are extremely topical.

PC   Two other similarities that I recognized in the work of Mario Botta and Louis Kahn are, on the one hand, the clear intellectual and tectonic definition of a building as an object with a beginning and an end, an exterior and an interior; on the other hand, I see the key to a great complexity of the works in achieving a strong relation to the context while at the same time emphasizing the individuality and the independent character of the buildings. Do I see that correctly?

MB   Like buildings, each person is unique. Each person has a personality, a character and a *Weltanschauung*, a general vision of the world. This analogy, as a precondition, in a way implies that a building cannot be arbitrary. The building contributes to something to which it does not have to respond explicitly. Parking spaces for Kahn become doors to the city, connecting elements in his university building become paths. Kahn invented things in his designs that were not asked for. In my opinion, this is important, it takes architecture further, to its maximum potential. It is not just a matter of function; a function that is genuinely functional is flexible, a certain-shaped room, synagogue or church can just as well be a restaurant or congress hall. A function can change, an institution cannot. Therefore, it also makes sense for an institution of collective gathering to express the collective. For me, this is a fundamental lesson of Kahn, from which he draws much of his skill. Interestingly, this lesson depicts a typical Scarpian paradox.
Which brings us to another exciting topic. Scarpa and Kahn were often juxtaposed as holy water and devil. Scarpa, as the one who brought a material to life, and Kahn as the one who thought exclusively in large dimensions. A reduction that does not correspond to the truth. I experienced how touched Kahn was by the monolithic stone shutters he looked at during a visit to centuries-old buildings on the island of Torcello. He, too, had a keen sense of detail and materiality.

Basilica Santa Maria Assunta
Torcello, Venice 1008

Scarpa and Kahn differed in the use of their architectural tools, but both had a poetic side when they gave materials an expressive quality.

PC   Honestly, you anticipated the question. I wanted to ask you to explain this simultaneous similarity and contrast between Kahn and Scarpa.

MB   I will tell you something very beautiful about Scarpa that may never have been written down. I met Carlo Scarpa for the very first time with Giuseppe Mazzariol in Venice in the Olivetti shop, which was still a construction site at the time. I really wanted to see the store, and when we came in, Scarpa walked up to us and started complaining: "Nowadays, you can't work anymore; Olivetti insists on the completion of the shop in a year. In a year!" It was a drama for him because he had been working on it for a decade.

The time and sensitivity that he spent on a project are reflected in the steps of the store's famous staircase. Its stone surfaces had been handcrafted up to this point with hammer and chisel. But recently, electric machines had been used for this purpose. He showed me the difference, which I could not see as much as I tried. To Scarpa it was painful; he saw that the manual roughening resulted in a velvet surface, while the machining, in contrast, resulted in a harder surface. A really small difference that only he could perceive through his sensitivity.

Every time I go to Venice, I look at the stones again and try unsuccessfully to see the difference. It is this oversensitivity that Carlo Scarpa had and that he shared with Kahn. In Kahn's buildings, it is found in the use of light; it is the true protagonist in the spaces, much more than geometry and more than design. The light generated the space.

PC   Let's go from the sensitivity of the two architects to the historical and academic context of the IUAV in Venice. Shortly before you started your studies, an eclectic team of teachers was summoned there by Giuseppe Samonà: Bruno Zevi, Ignazio Gardella, Carlo Scarpa, Franco Albini, Giancarlo De Carlo and others. Their successors, highly relevant figures such as Manfredo Tafuri, Carlo Aymonino, Aldo Rossi and Gianugo Polesello pushed the school towards a much more ideological

Carlo Scarpa
Olivetti Showroom
Venice 1957–1958

approach to teaching. Do you remember this development, which has enormous importance in the history of Italian architecture?

MB When I arrived in Venice in 1964, Venice was the centre of architectural thought, and the visionaries of this centre were the professors Samonà, Gardella, Scarpa, Giancarlo De Carlo and Vittorio De Feo.

PC Thinkers who also practised.

MB Building architects, just like Aldo Rossi. For me, it was charming, because as a young student I was able to learn that architecture can also be read as a part of the city. Until then, I had only been influenced by the German curriculum, whose biggest architectural problem was that no water could enter through the windows. Window profiles were drawn. Simplifying, one could call it the Nordic school, a school of good building that had become modern at that time, with the central figures being Karl Moser and Karl Friedrich Schinkel.
This was not an issue in Venice. Here a thematic examination of urban problems began, first through Giovanni Astengo and then through Luigi Piccinato. Thanks to them, the reading of the city as a fabric of architecture, which assumes a series of autonomous tasks, was established. Aldo Rossi's well-known position, in which he highlights the importance of urban monuments that stand out from the collective fabric of residential areas, continues this tradition. He shows that there are places that have a collective purpose, with symbolic, metaphorical values that are far more important than their functionality.
In the Nordic school, nobody spoke about the symbolic or metaphorical values of architecture. Through the design of kitchens and bedrooms, one had to find answers about what it means to eat or sleep well.
Later, there was a change at the university you mentioned, a generational change in which history, above all through the appointment of Tafuri, and ideology, through the ideas of the generation of 1968, became central themes.
Scarpa enjoyed little prestige during these years. I have seen Tafuri speak out against him more than once. Later, everything took a turn for the better.

PC Scarpa shaped the teaching at the University of Venice, Kahn at the University of Yale.
How has your own vision of an architectural curriculum developed, from the perception of these masters to the founding of the Accademia in Mendrisio?

MB It is a story full of anecdotes and a series of fortunate circumstances that led to the creation of a school at a national and academic level in the canton of Ticino, and that I could make a contribution.
Two years before this event, in 1991, I had been invited by the government to a discussion in which proposals were developed on how to prevent an overload of the architecture courses at ETH Zurich and EPF Lausanne through the increasing number of enrolments.
They asked me five questions, which I had not expected. One of them was whether it would be better to expand the established model of central Switzerland or adapt to a generalized system with a bachelor's or master's degree. I answered, albeit unprepared and relying on my Italian, or let's say humanistic culture. In my opinion, both the institution in Zurich, with its significant technical tradition originating from the Bauhaus, and the university in Lausanne, with its connections to the entire culture of French sociology and semiology, should not be touched. On the contrary, one could build another school in which the humanities are valued just as much as technical teaching. In my opinion, a problem at the beginning of the 1990s was that the polytechnic schools began with an enormous belief in technology, investing massively in computers and computer-aided work.
My idea was to found a school in contrast to this, in which no solutions were given, but questions were raised. In the end, the project was not immediately implemented. Two years later, however, a minister from Ticino talked about the foundation of an Italian university, so I went with my finished project to the government of the Italian speaking region of Switzerland and suggested to them to start with an architecture faculty that tied in with the great historical building culture of the region and carried it forward.
The big problem was that the Swiss universities were financed from a two billion Swiss franc pot distributed among the eight cantonal universities. The proposal of further splitting up the share could have proved suicidal!

So I had the ungrateful task of presenting the project to the rectors of the eight universities. Finally, everyone welcomed the international expert reports and assessed the project positively. They agreed, but with the belief that it would never be implemented.

A short time later, I was asked by the Ministry in Ticino when we would actually open the university, and I claimed in October of the same year, which we actually did. We didn't even have an address. The meetings took place on Sunday morning in my office, led by a motley crew. Everyone thought we would never make it.

The basic idea behind the university design is that, in order to respond to the complexity of modern culture, the integration of more humanistic subjects into education is inevitable.

The curriculum was extended to the subjects of History of Thought, Philosophy, History of Art, History of Architecture and Regional History. We appointed the philosopher Massimo Cacciari, the art historian Carlo Bertelli, the architect and historian Leonardo Benevolo and the philosopher and population geneticist Albert Jacquard for the subject of human ecology. We called them to the new university in Mendrisio to explain what it means to be human today. There were evening lectures with up to 500 people.

So, we started with the school, which not only offered solutions but also raised questions and addressed problems.

PC   It was a school that opened up in terms of content. One of the paradigms that was questioned there was the separation of culture and nature, which originated in German philosophy, and that now evolved into the dominating discussion on the Anthropocene. When the school started, the issue of the relations between mankind and ecology was already very relevant, whereas for other schools the main task was breaking the borders between disciplines, with a strong focus on technology, science and digital culture. Do you see any risk in the way architecture seems to rely on other disciplines today? Where do you see the benefit for concrete architectural projects in this development?

MB   It is not possible for me to give a universal answer to this question. Personally, I believe that nowadays every discipline draws its existential vigour from its limits and not from its centre. At the borders of disciplines, neurology, ecology or sociology, a development takes place.

In Mendrisio, we have organized conferences on topics that have led to astonishment. For example, we invited the neuroscientist Giacomo Rizzolatti, who discovered the mirror neurons responsible for the feeling of empathy. Many people asked me in advance what this had to do with architecture. Then, when Rizzolatti spoke about empathy in relation to space and territory that evening, these doubts were resolved. I believe that this reciprocal exchange serves a better understanding and is the basis to overcome complex problems.

PC Let's get back to Louis Kahn and his influence on your work. I have always wondered where the importance of symmetry in your oeuvre originated.

MB At the start, I never have a clear architectural idea; it develops later.

I often begin with the intention of not making a symmetrical project. I say to myself, even if I have to make a glass, I will not make it symmetrical. But then I start to work, and I finally find peace when I return to symmetry.

It is interesting, because a form is nothing intellectual or rational, but it serves to achieve a balance of light. For example, symmetry is a wonderful tool. If I'm looking for a light that is in balance twenty-four hours a day, I have to work with geometry. Andrea Palladio was capable of doing this, Albert Speer was not, yet both used geometry and symmetry. It is an instrument to be dealt with.

I think there must be a reason why you come back to something every time you try something new. It would be illogical not to use symmetry.

PC Do you agree with me that there are similar qualities in the interiors of the works of Kahn and Botta?

MB Architecture is space, and in it there are two dimensions that define it fundamentally. On the one hand, there is light. Let's take the Pantheon in Rome. It was a tomb, a market hall and a church, but beyond its functions, it was always the opening to the sky that gave the building its quality. On the other hand, there is the theme of monumentality. The architecture of the Pantheon draws its strength from within, not just from pure monumentality. Monumentality can be rhetorical and only finds its strength when it is able to carry within itself and pass on something of our collective past. We are able to reconstruct spaces, and it is easier for the brain if these spaces are clear and strong. I have always been fascinated by the inside of the Pantheon. We see only a part, but we recognize the whole. It is enough to see a fragment, and our brain reconstructs the overall geometric form. You know, without looking directly at it, in which direction you are moving, where the centre is and where the rear wall will come. That's an incredible ability.

Heidegger said that people live when they can orient themselves in the wholeness of a place. This also means that a person knows at what height he or she is in relation to the ground. It gives you a kind of security and ease. I believe that this is something we unconsciously seek in architecture.

PC   Did Louis Kahn work from a similar understanding of primary and secondary spaces with a serving function?

MB   Yes, they are part of a greater logic that makes orientation possible. But he liked to give this system an ambiguity, so he mixed them. I will give you an example. Once, he gave his students the task of designing a monastery, but the students didn't know how to start. A girl then had the idea of designing a monastery without hierarchies. She put forward the thesis that a church room was at least as important as a corridor. It is the idea of the ideal city where one joins a monastery to stay for a lifetime and discovers that each element has its own charm, its iconic power as a whole. Everybody had great expectations of the girl's project, which ultimately turned out to be a weak one. The thought, however, was strong, and sometimes Kahn reminds us, with a small disruption, that thoughts can be stronger than forms.

PC   Is there a material you prefer to work with?

MB   All materials are beautiful. Scarpa said you can use almost any material; you should only take into account that the shape of the building or the artifact will depend on that choice.

PC Do you know how Kahn himself worked, how the architect Kahn developed his concepts and ideas?

MB Kahn didn't develop his ideas in a team. It was a highly individual creative process in which he was able to control everything. Today, this way of working is rare.
I work in an office with my three children. Everyone takes on certain tasks.
Making architecture has changed a lot. I see it not only in school; the market has also become more profit-oriented and more complex. When I look at the drawings of my first houses, they consist of four sheets of paper. Now 400 drawings have to be developed for the same house, the themes of ecology, energy or, for example, transport have to be discussed separately.
This distracts the focus from the architectural facts and distorts them into issues of economy and risk avoidance. Kahn's thoughts in this respect are as topical as those of Palladio or Leon Battista Alberti were in the Renaissance. These key figures could correct certain errors. For me, Kahn is one of them. Despite everything, it is a good time to build. There are really good architects. Let's just take Tadao Andō or Álvaro Siza, for example. And even if building still seems like a long process, you have to realize that it used to take 200 years for a church to be built in its entirety. One did not see one's own design realized; today we are fortunate to see it.

Mario Botta was born in Mendrisio in 1943 and began his professional career in Lugano in 1970. He has taught internationally through lectures, seminars and courses at many architecture schools in Europe, Asia, the United States and Latin America. He is an honorary member of many cultural institutions and has been awarded honorary degrees at universities in Argentina, Greece, Romania, Bulgaria, Brazil and Switzerland. In 1996 he was one of the prime movers and founders of the Academy of Architecture in Mendrisio, where he taught until 2018 and which he led as Dean of the Academy from 2002 to 2003 and from 2011 to 2013.

Pippo Ciorra was born in Formia in 1955 and works as an architect, critic and professor as well as being an author and curator. From 1996 to 2012 he was a member of the editorial staff of the Italian architecture magazine *Casabella* and is the author of numerous publications. Ciorra teaches design and theory at SAAD (University of Camerino) and is director of the international PhD program "Villard d'Honnecourt" (IUAV). Pippo Ciorra is a member of CICA (International Committee of Architectural Critics) and advisor to the Gold Medal for Italian Architecture awards. He has also curated national and international exhibitions. Since 2009 he has been the leading curator of the MAXXI (Museo nazionale delle arti del XXI secolo) in Rome. He has published, among others, *Botta, Eisenman, Gregotti, Hollein: Museums*, 1991, as editor, and *Nuova architettura italiana*, 2000, as well as *La metropoli dopo*, 2002, as co-editor.

Louis I. Kahn was born in 1901 in Kuressaare and died in 1974 in New York. From 1906 he lived in the USA, where he studied architecture at the University of Pennsylvania from 1920 to 1924. From 1947 to 1957 he taught as professor of architecture at the Yale School of Architecture and until 1974 at the School of Design of the University of Pennsylvania. He received numerous awards including the AIA Gold Medal and the RIBA Gold Medal. His most important works include the Phillips Exeter Academy Library, New Hampshire, 1972, the Salk Institute for Biological Studies in La Jolla, 1965, and the National Parliament House in Dhaka, begun in 1963 and completed in 1983, after Kahn's death.

Momoyo Kaijima and Lise Juel meet to talk about Jørn Utzon. Kaijima and Juel already worked together on the exhibition *Atelier Bow-Wow: Learning from Utzon* in Aalborg in 2013. At that time, they also had the opportunity to visit some of Utzon's buildings together.

LJ When was your first encounter with Utzon, and has your relationship towards his work changed with time?

MK I am not specialized on Utzon. The first building I visited was the Sydney Opera House. I couldn't find any photographs at that period, but I visited it and I joined the guided tour of the building. And then the second time, I went to a very popular classical concert with music from the eighteenth century to the twentieth century with Yoshiharu Tsukamoto, my partner. I found that twentieth-century music and space are very related to each other. The size of the space and the ambitions of the room remind me that music is one of the functions, but it's also a real spatial effect. Utzon's architecture is constantly making me think that he had an idea of how to use and spend time in this space. This kind of understanding of space is a continuous inspiration for me.

LJ You did a drawing of the Sydney Opera House for the exhibition in Aalborg in 2013. You drew that iconic building with all sorts of life activities in it. This meticulous way of drawing, this focal point within your work, is it more than a tool, more than understanding the situation within the site? What happens when you draw?

MK Of course, the building itself is interesting as an architectural element. The Sydney Opera House is a tall and symbolic volume, but it also has a surrounding public space. Besides the form and scale of the building, the behaviour of people in that space is important. How do they behave in different climatic situations, different seasons and periods of the day? Maybe there is more activity in the mornings and the evenings. Or what happens if there is a concert or not? You can visit the Sydney Opera House and observe the surroundings and the behaviour of people for a day or even a week. It might bring more input. But I think that this kind of drawing always includes expectation, prediction and imagination. Jørn Utzon's example, and drawing it that way, makes us learn about the building. Mainly, however, we learn about the effect the building has on people. I think that is very important for architects to learn.

LJ Yes, I agree, especially thinking about Jørn Utzon's manifesto "The Innermost Being of Architecture" from 1948.

Jørn Utzon
Can Lis
Mallorca 1973

Or the creation process of the exterior dining space of Can Lis, which is one of Utzon's many stories. According to him, he observed the construction site and the place the workers actually took their lunch, and then he decided to place there the exterior dining space. This is somehow the beginning of the life of the building and the life within the building. How do you think it actually works?

MK Somehow it reminds me of camping. For example, on our construction sites, carpenters and workers always find interesting and good ways to rest and have lunch related to the site and weather conditions. And sometimes we use that intuitive ability that even animals have in our projects. It is an important part of an honest way of life.

LJ Taking the keyword "honest", I would like to come back to drawing. For many architects, a drawing is rarely honest. It is this dream that is never fulfilled when the building actually stands there. But the way you are handling it, drawing is a more objective tool documenting what is really there. I see that as a really interesting approach and related to how Utzon used it. Although he was a wonderful drawer, drawing in itself did not interest him. His drawings show exactly how things are done. Detailing in 1:1, the real formats of things and the proportion of the full-scale space were his interest. When he planned Can Lis, he spent years studying typologies of stone buildings and taking pictures of combining stones. And then he used his sons as columns on site to figure out how to find the right positions. I was wondering whether you do similar things to develop your projects?

MK Of course, we try to. Maybe not 1:1, but first we visit the site and try to imagine or understand the space itself, the character, the feeling or even the climate. And normally the sites are surrounded by buildings. So, it is important to refer to them because they may stay longer than our project. Some of them are not well-designed, but even so, they play a role. To imagine a typology, you have to look at the neighbours' typology. We do not just want to build one symbolical building; we want to interact with the neighbourhood, collecting the common spirit and behaviour and giving an answer to it on our site.

LJ That reminds me a bit of a story that I heard. There was a visitor that lived a couple of days with Jørn Utzon in Can Lis, and then when she left, she said, "What's wrong with comfort?" And this brings me from Can Lis and its ritualized events to the architectural framework. But before that framing of architecture can be done, you investigate behaviour and the site. And that brings you to the spatial solution.

MK I think in Can Lis we can reduce the framework of some spaces to very simple and fundamental architectural elements, like a roof and pillars. There are more details, but those fundamental elements create these kinds of gap spaces, which make the difference.

LJ Those archaic architectural elements create a kind of timeless universality and quality. Are there, in comparison, certain elements you are particularly interested in?

MK We are also interested in architectural elements like the eaves, the roof, the pillar and the stair. In our designs, we use those elements and create different sizes and proportions between them. If you relate to design elements just in a very functional way, you lose the freedom of the element. But when we think about the effect that elements with different sizes and proportions create, elements can have more freedom. If we design a window with enough depth, we can use it in many ways. Or pillars with enough space in between can be used as places to sleep or relax.

LJ I remember a Japanese photographer who stayed in Can Lis for about three days, and he talked about the architectural phenomenon that spaces in Can Lis always point you to a new space somehow. He said that in Japan you have a specific architectural expression for that way of organizing space.

MK Yes, the diagonals, like in Can Lis, are what we are interested in. Not only to go straight, but also to offer multiple directions, also visually. To not limit the usage, we can do this or that or we can look here or there. But that makes it difficult to take pictures of our work. A picture can never show the full space and its elements. But a person in that space, without

Jørn Utzon
Can Lis
Mallorca 1973

looking backwards, feels light, heat or sound coming through the window in the back. We experiment with that sense and it gives us more dynamic spatial ideas.

LJ Particularly here, there is a huge similarity between your work and Utzon's work. It's impossible to capture it. The medium film works best when you go through Utzon's buildings.

MK Yes, but visitors can understand his architectural intention.

LJ It always should be the best when you visit. You must have visited architectural works where the photos are fantastic, but then you go there, and you think the photos were actually better. It is never like that with Jørn Utzon's works.

MK Yes, I think that is a very remarkable part.

LJ But I don't know why. Is it because of starting inside out? He did that in a way. Of course, the shape of his buildings has importance, but still, the life he imagined was the first step before using the pencil. And you do almost the same thing.

MK Yes, I think he enjoyed the process of designing, right? We also like it: the thinking, reading and discussing. Sometimes you see an interesting construction detail in a book, or by talking to people you come up with ideas and you are able to learn from them. We also try to encourage and motivate our carpenters to do even better work than they already do. And sometimes that leads to productive tensions between them and us.

LJ That's true, and I've heard that at later works of Jørn Utzon, he held a speech for the workers on the site. He told the plumbers how important it is that the veins of the buildings are beautifully exposed and that they are part of the breathing of the building. You need everybody to work with you to create a masterpiece.

MK The energy and passion of architects, workers and clients working hard together lead to a much better quality of building. Teamwork is an interesting part of architecture. It is not only one person making a building, but many. Architecture needs people, and, of course, time and resources, as well as the joy of constructing together.

Utzon, for example, was interested in the yacht and sailing boat culture and teamwork-related sport. In Japan, we often have soccer teams in offices and universities. We play just for fun, but doing it makes us learn about communication and people's characters. Somehow, it is comparable to constructing.

LJ And that works out well. If you build several buildings with the same carpenter, he knows you very well. I know one that I work with from time to time, and it's really nice to be challenged from his perspective. He would say, "You should change this detail or that one."

MK Or the carpenter even complains or criticises me. But when I manage to convince him to do something my way, by the end he mostly agrees and says, "It was such a hard job for us, but I really appreciate your proposal."

If carpenters work with architects, and they establish a good understanding with each other, they are normally also convinced and are very satisfied with the result. They might even enjoy the difference, and what they have learned from the experience. Utzon tried to create his architecture in a different way from the usual, and it was definitely a big challenge.

LJ Yes, absolutely. Josep Montserrat, the original builder of Can Lis, was later part of our restoration team and did a lot of repairs. And when he talks about his relationship to Utzon, he seems like a second father to him who revolutionised his way of thinking. So, it can be an extremely overwhelming and enriching experience for the workers if they really are into these wonderful projects.

MK When we started our career, constructors were mostly older than us. And I had to convince and even beg them to do things. That was kind of hard. Nowadays, there is a younger generation of carpenters who are maybe not more skilled but more flexible. They are open to ideas instead of doing things just the traditional way. We enjoy the work with different generations and different point of views.

LJ This is about linking different strengths. It can be good for architecture when you find compromises between traditional and new ways. Does this network of different actors and the input you get from it form your own projects?

MK Yes! Of course, in the twenty-first century we can find everything on the Internet, but in architecture it is still so important to work with that network. To bring in new skills, methods or materials.

LJ We have talked a lot about the similarities between your work and Utzon's work. Why don't we look at the differences now? Sometimes, you feel related to somebody, but there are parts that you don't understand. Is there anything about which you would say, "I simply don't understand why he did that?"

MK When I first visited the Sydney Opera House, I didn't know why Utzon was so fascinated by precast concrete. He used those big concrete shells, which were, of course, at that period a new technology. But in Japan, concrete structures are made mostly on-site rather than being prefabricated. It is much cheaper than prefabrication. So, that was really the first thing I thought when I saw the Sydney Opera House. But then we had the chance to build the Four Boxes Gallery for the Krabbesholm Højskole. And they wanted us to make a building out of concrete. So, we visited several concrete factories, and, in fact, there is a highly developed concrete prefabrication in Denmark. Maybe it's because of climatic or quality issues or because of the system of construction. And in Japan, because of narrow streets and for other reasons, we do not use prefabricated concrete so much. In the beginning, it was hard for me to understand that it is a cultural difference.

LJ How did you, in your contemporary and cultural setting, see Utzon's Kingo Houses as a housing project when we visited them together?

MK We don't have those repetitive single housing components as much in Japan. Social housing is mostly public, and there is a lot of interest in single private housing. In Denmark, there instead exists a production system of corporate social housing that does not only include poor people. I was fascinated by that. The Kingo Houses open up to connect to their surroundings and share spaces. On the other hand, they give a nice separation and individuality. Japanese houses are much narrower and have small gardens. The Kingo Houses are in some kind of park.

LJ Danish parcels are usually highly orthogonally structured and have an individual garden. So, the Kingo Houses were kind of revolutionary, even in Denmark. Utzon created a small society where you could take it all the way in.

MK That would be so difficult in Japan because of property issues and finding so many people to support that incredible idea.

LJ Another interesting layer of this project is the inspiration taken from indigenous building structures, as in the Atlas Mountains of Morocco. The Kingo Houses have beautiful spaces, but I don't know how much of the life within them was part of the design. Jørn Utzon writes in his manifesto about the alliance of architects and society, but in my opinion, he is more spatial than societal. And it is also a question of the time he was working in and the modern point of view.

MK In the 1960s and 1970s, many Japanese architects made apartment blocks trying to anticipate the communal space. For example, Kiyonori Kikutake made a big shared terrace in front of the apartments, but, unfortunately, this did not work well because of having to share the terrace. It is difficult for Japanese people to know how to behave in shared spaces. It is very different from Japanese traditional spaces like the *Engawa*. In that period, a lot of architects tried to bring different international lifestyles into their own culture. I read several times that northern architects admired or were even obsessed by the idea of bringing Greek or Roman culture into the north. This fascination for a different culture also brings contradictions. The courtyards of the Kingo Houses are very Mediterranean, but with a big distance between them. Although the buildings are touching each other,

Jørn Utzon
Kingo Houses
Helsingør 1958

Jørn Utzon
Kingo Houses
Helsingør 1958

in-between there are big gardens and the loggia spaces; maybe originally, real loggia spaces were enclosed. I was thinking, "Ah, Mediterranean culture has become winter gardens in Denmark."

LJ But maybe it's more adapted to actual life in Denmark than the Nordic architecture. Sverre Fehn once said that the Nordic architects have forgotten space and focus on the detail instead. Utzon is not one of them, but there is some truth in it. So, in some ways he succeeds in transferring it to the Danish way of life, even though it's Mediterranean. And he lived for many years in Spain and Hawaii, so that's part of him, too.

MK I think that the transformation of the loggia to a winter garden is a good innovation from him. It's just single-glazing, but it gives people a nice warm space in winter. It is a good observation of the original loggia. He did this kind of scientific analysis and tested it.

LJ And he understood the living conditions of the place. That seems banal, but it was of extreme importance to his work. And what also strikes me is the archaicness of his structures that are robust enough in order to be transformed over time to frame new and different situations.

MK They are simple structures like a wall and a roof. In Japanese cases, the roof and pillars are important, but in European culture the wall is first and the roof is second. Of course, walls can be different in the southern regions, but the masonry construction system is the same. Within this construction system, Utzon was always honest about the material representation of gravity.

LJ But he insisted on the roof. That was extremely important for his architecture. He also spoke about organic growth, the way he conceives his buildings. Of course, that is inspired by the Katsura temple plans. That is how he worked, in my opinion. You also work with these spatial flows more than with the building as such. Is that the way you think?

MK If we have a lot of space, of course we try to do that, but most of the projects have a compact size.

LJ From my point of view, I do not think it is a matter of compactness. Compact or not, I think we can still conclude that Jørn Utzon and you both work with space as the essential and initial element in the creation of a place, where the architectural framework at a later stage follows the initial spatial narrative.

Momoyo Kaijima founded Atelier Bow-Wow in Tokyo together with Yoshiharu Tsukamoto in 1992. She studied architecture at the Tokyo Institute of Technology, where she received her doctorate in 1999. She has been a visiting professor at numerous universities, including Harvard in 2003 and ETH Zurich from 2005 to 2007. Since 2017 she has been head of the Chair of Architectural Behaviourology at ETH Zurich. She has realized numerous public and residential buildings, including the Nora House, 2006, the Four Boxes Gallery, 2009, and the BMW Guggenheim Lab, 2011. Momoyo Kaijima has also published several books, including two volumes of *Graphic Anatomy—Atelier Bow-Wow*, 2007/2014, and *Behaviorology*, 2010.

Lise Juel was born in Denmark in 1969 and studied architecture at the Royal Academy of Fine Arts, School of Architecture in Copenhagen. In 2010 she founded her studio Atelier Lise Juel after having worked for a range of leading architectural practices in Denmark, including Kim Utzon Architects, where she was chief designer, and the Utzon Center, where she was lead architect in collaboration with Jørn Utzon. Lise Juel is Associate Professor at The Royal Academy of Fine Arts, School of Architecture, where she has been teaching since 2002. Due to her collaboration with Jørn Utzon, Lise Juel was commissioned to restore Can Lis in 2012 and one of the Kingo Houses in 2013. Furthermore, she initiated the collaboration on an exhibition with Atelier Bow-Wow at the Utzon Center in 2013.

Jørn Utzon was born in Copenhagen in 1918 and died there in 2008. He studied architecture at the Royal Academy of Fine Arts in Copenhagen from 1937 to 1942. After his studies, he worked for Gunnar Asplund, Alvar Aalto and Frank Lloyd Wright, amongst others. In 1950 he opened his own architectural practice, which he ran until his death. The term "additive architecture" is based on his approach of describing his architecture on the basis of growth patterns in nature. In 1957 he won the competition to design the Sydney Opera House, the construction of which brought him international recognition. Other important buildings by Jørn Utzon include the Kingo Houses in Helsingør, 1958, Bagsværd Church, 1968, and Can Lis on Mallorca, 1971. In 2003 Jørn Utzon was awarded the Pritzker Prize.

on Walter Gropius
László Moholy-Nagy

with Olaf Nicolai

In their lecture and conversation about Walter Gropius and László Moholy-Nagy, Donatella Fioretti and Olaf Nicolai reflect on their engagement with the two great figures of the Bauhaus, also in relation to their own work, which manifests itself in the collaboration on the New Masters' Houses in Dessau.

DF Our conversation is not only about architects on architects, but also about artists on artists. The architect Walter Gropius and the artist László Moholy-Nagy are the protagonists we dealt with at the project for the New Masters' Houses in Dessau.
My encounter with Gropius was rather accidental. Unlike other architects, such as Lina Bo Bardi, Gunnar Asplund or Sigurd Lewerentz, his work has not shaped me. My knowledge of Gropius' work is based on the knowledge I acquired during my studies. But as an architect, it didn't really move me. I see the importance of his work much more as a promoter, as a mediator, than as an architect, even if he created some complex and undoubtedly important buildings. He participated in the November Revolution, was involved in the Workers' Council for Art, which was an association of revolutionary artists based on the council movement, and founded the Bauhaus in Weimar in 1919. He had a very keen sense of time and worked with it. Gropius as an architect is not an important reference for my own work. However, it is a different situation with you and László Moholy-Nagy, isn't it?

ON We also met through the collaboration on the Masters' Houses. I find Moholy-Nagy fascinating for a similar reason as you described for Gropius. You could almost call him a propagandist. He realizes how important external communication is, what it means to establish a brand. There is a very nice film that he made on behalf of Sigfried Giedion about the CIAM Congress in Athens. The congress, which should have taken place in the Soviet Union, was held on a ship due to the political situation in Russia. Together with Le Corbusier, Giedion convinced a Greek shipowner to make a ship available to them as a conference venue. This film hasn't been shown often because Giedion thought everyone would think they were on holiday, having fun and not working seriously. Moholy-Nagy was very aware of what he was doing. He captured an atmosphere in this film that introduces an attitude to life that goes far beyond a classic concept of architecture. In coordination with Gropius, he did massive public relations work for the external impact of the Bauhaus, for example, by pursuing the idea of establishing the Bauhaus books as a series. More than fifty titles were planned, and there was really nothing that should not have appeared under the label "Bauhaus". There were titles on homoeopathy, esoterics and applied physics. Everyone who seemed important was invited to make a Bauhaus book. Or simply only once listed. It was a massive advertising campaign to establish Bauhaus as the epitome of "contemporary". From the outset, you don't leave the interpretation to others but control it yourself. I found it remarkable how Moholy-Nagy used it to create a corporate identity. Something that has determined architecture ever since. Important architects, without thinking about their corporate identity and branding in the background, cannot be understood, not even economically. And I also find Moholy-Nagy impressive as an artist, especially his experiments with light and film, abstract forms that he also understood politically.

DF To what extent can abstraction be political?

ON In El Lissitzky's *Cabinet of Abstraction*, the film *Battleship Potemkin* ran alongside one of Hans Richter's abstract films—parallel. I saw this for the first time at the Van Abbemuseum in Eindhoven. Both films comment on each other, change the view. In Sergei Eisenstein's film, the montage technique comes to the fore, the treatment of details, the break with linearity. The revolutionary moment is not the content, it is the form. It calls up options, for different perception, different behaviour. This is where the political begins for me.

DF The invitation in 2009 to participate in the competition for the New Masters' Houses in Dessau was an occasion for us to intensively examine Gropius' architecture and world of thought. This immersion in the thoughts of another architect is relatively strange and sometimes alienating.
In 1919 Walter Gropius founded the Bauhaus in Weimar with the intention of establishing the best art school of the time there. Six years later, the Bauhaus was dissolved in Weimar under political pressure from the Thuringian state, which was increasingly dominated by National Socialist forces. But it was able to settle in Dessau in the same year thanks to the open-mindedness and initiative of Mayor Fritz Hesse. Dessau offered fertile ground on which art, industry and politics could meet and interact. Walter Gropius hoped that his collaboration with entrepreneurs such as Hugo Junkers would lead to the "unity of art and technology" he propagated. The location of

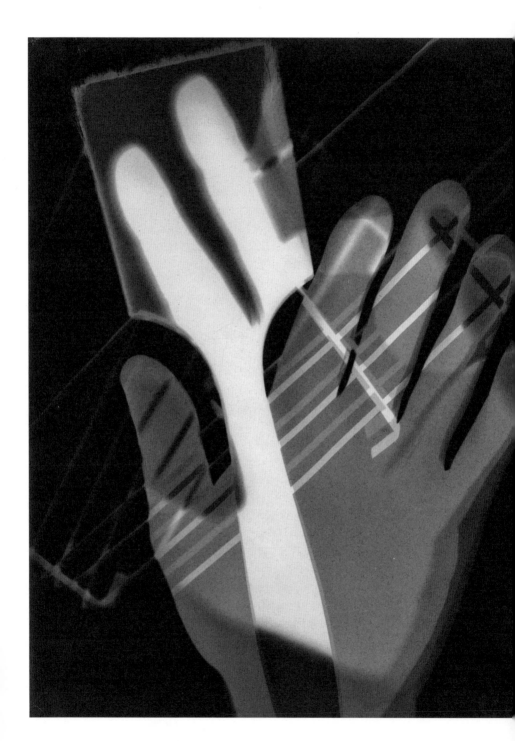

László Moholy-Nagy
Photogram
1926

the Bauhaus in the culturally remote Dessau prompted Gropius to create special features in order to attract the best artists to the Bauhaus.

It is said that during a walk through a beautiful grove, Gropius convinced the mayor to build these houses for the Bauhaus masters; houses with studios where artists such as Moholy-Nagy, Albers, Klee and Feininger could live and work.

At the same time, however, Gropius skilfully used the houses for advertising purposes, for example for Junkers, as one of the great sponsors of the Bauhaus. Film documentaries show how, in her private kitchen, Ise Gropius explains the advantages of the new kitchen and the relief it offers for women's work. These targeted advertising campaigns served to propagate their own architecture and the Bauhaus idea as a whole.

A contemporary criticism of Gropius was that the director's house he designed and inhabited—in stark contrast to the ideological approaches of the Bauhaus—corresponded to a luxurious villa. Following the traditional villa typologies, there was a garage, a caretaker's apartment, a wine cellar and a private garden shielded by a wall from the street and the views of the neighbours.

By comparing photographs of the bathroom, one discovers a clear case of image manipulation. The bourgeois marble of the washbasin was retouched in the published photograph because it did not fit in with the democratic image of the Bauhaus.

Image manipulations and skilful perspectives in the photographs of Lucia Moholy, who staged the Masters' Houses as modern, abstract compositions of cubic elements, were intended to propagate the ideas of the Bauhaus.

The materials available to Gropius for the construction of the houses probably did not offer him the static possibilities for the desired architectural expression. At the director's house, where the volume was to protrude over the terrace, he was forced to provide two supports. To conceal this, he uses a dark glass cladding. The houses were photographed by Lucia Moholy in such a way that the reflection of the glass almost makes the static elements disappear.

The floor plans, on the other hand, are more conventional than those of other contemporary architects, who had a much more radical understanding of living.

ON The times since the Masters' Houses came into exis-
tence have been politically very diverse. How did this affect the
houses?

DF The interesting thing about the Masters' Houses is that
they existed in four completely different political systems: first
in the Weimar Republic, then under National Socialism, followed by the era of the GDR and finally in the period after the
fall of the Wall.

During National Socialism, the Bauhaus became the epitome of "degenerated art". The buildings would certainly have
been demolished if the demolition had not been seen as a
questionable political decision due to the housing shortage in
the 1930s.

Instead, attempts were made to remodel the apartments so that
they corresponded more closely to the *Heimatstil* propagated by
the government. Moreover, like many modern buildings, the
houses did not work well climatically. For this reason, in addition to numerous changes, the windows were reduced in size.

Towards the end of the Second World War, the director's house
and the semi-detached house, originally occupied by Moholy-
Nagy, were destroyed in air raids on Dessau. The plinth, cellar, garage and parts of the garden wall of House Gropius were
preserved.

In the 1950s, a house with a saddle roof, the so-called House
Emmer, was placed on the plinth. The wall with the drinking
hall designed by Mies van der Rohe was demolished at the end
of the 1960s. In the GDR period, there was no real understanding of the Bauhaus, and it was considered elitist and formal-
istic. Accordingly, the Bauhaus buildings in Dessau were not
maintained, which meant that they were in a ruinous state after
the fall of communism.

It was only after the reunification of Germany that the houses were rediscovered. Their cultural potential and their effect
as tourist catalysts were recognized. Between 1992 and 2000,
the houses Feininger, Kandinsky/Klee and Muche/Schlem-
mer were restored according to different concepts. There have
been long discussions about how to deal with House Emmer
and the half of the house originally occupied by Moholy-Nagy.
Questions were asked about the preservation or demolition
of House Emmer as well as whether the houses Gropius and
Moholy-Nagy should be reconstructed or not.

Walter Gropius
House Gropius
Dessau 1926

Walter Gropius
House Gropius
Dessau 1926

`ON` How did you position yourself politically, but also architecturally?

`DF` The task in the competition was not to design a building on the basis of a programme, as is usually the case, but rather to adopt an attitude towards the Masters' Houses as a whole.

That was an unusually open programme. Ulrike Wendland, head of restorations, and Philipp Oswalt, then director of the Bauhaus Foundation, spoke of an urban repair instead of a reconstruction.

Restorations are about restoring lost parts of a piece of art if they are important for being able to read the piece of art as a whole. These parts should remain recognizable as additions. In the restoration of paintings or frescoes, there is the well-known "Tratteggio technique", in which lost parts are restored in a reduced colour intensity using a dash technique so that the entire picture can be experienced again. Hardly visible from a distance, the additions can only be seen on closer inspection.

The idea was to transfer the Tratteggio technique to architecture and urban planning. This measure was intended to make the entire settlement readable and experienceable again.

The question we asked ourselves was what filling material could be used for the missing fragments.

Against the wave of reconstruction currently taking place in Germany, we found the task of finding an attitude and a strategy a very courageous approach, especially for a small town like Dessau. The choice against the politically consensual reconstruction of a monument and for the difficult path of a conceptual strategy was quite extraordinary.

A reconstruction in the classical, philological sense was also out of the question because of the insufficiency of existing documents. While discussing the existing documents on the houses, we came across an album with photos of the Masters' Houses that Ise Gropius had collected during her time in Dessau.

We found that, in addition to the factual-historical and iconographic levels of the Masters' Houses, there is an intimate level that is transported via these photos. When we looked at them, it became clear to us that it could not be our task to document a historical condition and make settlement fragments readable again. We were, rather, confronted with the difficult and deceitful topic of memory.

We regarded forgetting as an inevitable part of remembering. Memories live from inaccuracy and fuzziness. We could not ignore these inaccuracies; we had to work with this blur to find the right tone for the task.

Building a presence and, at the same time, evoking an absence is not easy in architecture. Looking for examples that could help us along the path of conception, the works of Hiroshi Sugimoto and Thomas Demand came to mind. In the photo series *Architecture*, Sugimoto picks up icons of architecture with a double infinity setting that causes the uniform blurring of all contours. Sugimoto, who normally works very precisely and with a high level of detail, moves here to the limit of recognizability. With the series, he explores the question of how far one can manipulate an image until the depicted object becomes unrecognizable.

Demand also works with images. These are images that we know from the press. These images, as information carriers of collective memory, are manipulated by the transfer into various media, abstracted and alienated by the conscious omission of details. The spaces depicted are not immediately recognizable as models. Images are created that cause irritation and, at the same time, create an extraordinary atmospheric density through the rigorous precision of the operation.

Sugimoto's and Demand's work has helped us to understand better the nature of the Dessau task. What we were looking for was a project that evokes absence and presence, a project that creates distance over proximity and precisely deals with blur.

ON   How did you transfer the theme into architecture?

DF   While working on the project, we split the building into two operational components—the outer shell and the internal structure. The shell is a monolithic casting. The dimensions and proportions of the structures, as well as the original position of the openings, are adopted to refer to the former urban situation of the complex.

In order to reduce the details, and thus simplify the abstraction of the structures, we have decided to use only one single material and have produced the shell as a monolithic casting of insulating concrete. Since the sensuality, which is primarily conveyed by the material and the details, is an essential aspect of architecture for us, we had built a 1:1 sample. This way we were able to check the effect of different formworks and details. And we were able to determine the balance between abstraction and sensuality. The construction also made it possible to build the cantilevered corner without the reflecting supports of Gropius. We, therefore, took the liberty of following Gropius' actual idea and dispensing with the supports.

The windows that most clearly indicate the changed use of the houses are flush with the facade. The translucent glass protects the exhibition rooms from direct sunlight and allows the contours of the outer environment to be perceived schematically from the inside only.

The glass for the large-format openings in the outer shell was also important to us. Its dimensions and positions were taken from the original building, but its appearance should correspond to the abstract expression of the shell. Our original idea was to cast the windows from glass or epoxy resin. But that would have cost a fortune.

The glass is flush with the concrete facade and the construction is deeply hidden in the joint. A white coating of glass paint was applied to the six-millimetre-thick panes of white glass. The two panes were laminated in the oven and finally installed as double insulating glazing. The process produced a moving depth and body to the glass.

The slightly irregular glass panes absorb the changing light conditions of the surroundings and create a lively surface through distorted reflections.

A soft, homogeneous light floods the interior; the surroundings are perceived as shadowy. Weather and orientation influence the transparency of the glass and cause subtle fluctuations between interior and exterior space.

Concrete and glass are the defining materials of the outer shell. Both are reduced to a minimal expression that questions the familiar appearance of the context. This operation supports the abstract nature of urban repair.

We understand the internal structure as an overall structure and have inserted it as a plastic body into the cavity of the interior. The motif of the cupboard integrated into the wall is taken up here as a formative element of Bauhaus architecture. The compositional lines of the original house are fragmentarily recorded and depicted as oversized furniture. This wooden structure, which was called an "artifact" by the project participants throughout the planning and construction process, houses not only the technical installations but also the circulation.

The spatial sequence of the historical house is hinted at in the artifact, but not reproduced one-to-one. The reduction of the house to two elements allows multi-layered readings. This solution is to be understood as a suggestion to supplement the image of the house in thought itself. At the same time, it develops an independent composition, a tension between massive shell and wooden installation. The relationship between artifact and shell has been studied using numerous working models.

The artifact was created in a kind of reverse archaeology. In the normal archaeological process, one finds pieces that are then joined to form a whole. In this case, we had the whole thing and reduced it to a fragment.

With Philipp Oswalt, we talked about the artifact, its function and design. He suggested working on the theme with an artist, Olaf Nicolai. At the time, we couldn't imagine what an art concept would look like that could cope with the materiality, dimensions and proportions of the houses—after all, the houses are very small.

ON   At this point I joined the project. When we met and these artifacts stood there, I noticed the caution architects have in dealing with visual artists, because they themselves think very figuratively. And, in fact, after you introduced me to the concept, I didn't really know at first what was going to happen because it was a strong sculptural setting. The houses seen from outside, as well as the artifacts inside, are clearly modelled sculptural elements with defined proportions designed with the help of images. This interested me—the function of the picture. Those things were very much discussed at that time, for example, in the case of the Berlin Palace reconstruction. Unfortunately, something has prevailed there that can now be admired in the form of the newly built palace. A little joke of history—in a project that otherwise hasn't much fun to offer—is the fact that there will now be two balconies: the historic balcony of the palace where Karl Liebknecht proclaimed the Republic, which was attached to the GDR State Council Building, and the copy for the reconstruction of the palace facade. Against this background, I found your attitude very interesting, not to make a complete repositioning but to work with an entirely different kind of reconstruction. It does not make one forget the temporality that would have been hidden by a simple reconstruction. That's why I also liked the houses from the GDR that stood there until now. In their way of confrontation, they tell much more about the sensual and political constellations than image-supported reconstructions.

The architects' cautious fear of the visual artist was noticeable here at first, and I asked myself, "What can I do here?" It was about the surface of these artifacts inside the building, built as planked wooden constructions. Those walls face the concrete interior walls of the shells. This was a confrontation of two materials. That was the point where I wanted to start. What would actually happen on the surface of the artifacts if I didn't work on them? It was said that they would be plastered. When one speaks about Bauhaus today, the term of function and the conceptual clarity of the designs are often emphasized. A closer look reveals that many aesthetic decisions were made without following such a clear logic and that functional argumentation was only added afterwards—as you mentioned with the example of the bathrooms.

This is where I started: there is a surface of plaster and a disguised body. On the basis of the geometric grid of its wooden construction, I only wanted to use plaster as surface material. I suggested defining four different plaster grains and design patterns based on the grid, which would then be executed in plaster. What most people probably couldn't see at the time of my proposal was the effect that produced the diffuse light of the special glasses that you had proposed for the outer shell of the houses.

DF   How did you test the effect of light?

ON   I tested it on studies—folded papers on which I placed white tones to see how the surface could be modelled by light reflection. These studies are called *Le pigment de la lumière*. On paper, however, it's not what you'd expect when you hear pigment. It is white gouache on white paper. When plastering, through the different grains, the light refracts at different angles, and these make a play of light and shadow appear. Not only the surfaces themselves with different grains of plaster play a role, but also the movement of the sun and clouds, the times of day and seasons, as well as light sources inside the rooms and the movement of people. Your windows in this work are particularly interesting because when you are inside, the outside world is only present as shadow through the opaque panes. If you look in from the outside, you get a cinematic effect. Inside, there are shadow projections that are triggered by various movements. In principle, this is what László Moholy-Nagy was concerned with in his experiments on the representation of light, in which abstraction and figuration play together.

This work is difficult to grasp from photographs. I asked the photographer Heidi Specker to document it together with me. In the sequence of her pictures, you can see how the surfaces change.

DF In order to realize this idea, we had to find craftsmen who knew how to create the edges of different surfaces so precisely and clearly that they would collide seamlessly, even without using angle profiles. We were able to test it on samples. The seamless application of the textures was truly a masterpiece of craftsmanship. It was fantastic to see how the surfaces change with light and movement. With this subtle kind of surface design and its effect in the light, we wanted to capture the spirit of the original architecture. At the same time, it is an independent work with a clear statement. However, one has to look very closely to perceive this effect. Many visitors overlook this.

ON The fact that the work is not perceived at first is a nice compliment. Alongside the perception through light, the attempt to think about time plays a role within this work. It is temporal phenomena that one experiences, light and movement. When one moves through the rooms, the work changes continuously. And the aspect of time also corresponded to the original idea of using the rooms. Philipp Oswalt had the idea that the spaces be used as libraries and for exhibitions, not in a traditional way, but as spaces defined by dance or music. These walls are notations from which pieces of music could develop. There are options, but unfortunately there is no money, and no one is conceptionally working on it. This is the status that fixes the work as a mural for the moment. Yet it could be like a screen for very different interventions. But that still can happen.

Olaf Nicolai
Le pigment de la lumière, Studie 8
2014

DF You talked about the relationship of your work to architecture. How does this work relate to Moholy-Nagy?

ON In the 1930s, Moholy-Nagy very clearly stated in the manifesto "From Pigment to Light" ("Du pigment à la lumière") the renunciation of traditional painterly solutions in favour of the design of spaces with moving light sources. Interestingly, as early as the 1940s, he turned away from this trend because he was too dependent on capital and industry. At that time, he stopped experimenting with light, believing that he was becoming what he called the "slave of both the technical and the material, the plaything of random patrons", that only the artist's studio was still a place of independent design—and he started painting again. From the 1940s, there were no photos, no films from him anymore; there were oil paintings instead.

DF You use very different media for your works. What is your interest and what is your approach?

ON I try to concentrate on what the object facing me is, or the situation I enter, and what they predefine. I wonder what logic they have. From this, I develop a kind of answer, an objection, which takes up that logic. It was the same with the work for the Masters' Houses. I didn't want to juxtapose pictoriality with other pictoriality but to work with what architecture dictates. And in a way that can be traced back relatively far to the specification itself. It refers to existing structures and given material. And, of course, the investigation of how the surfaces of the artifacts work in space, so that certain refractions of light are really good because the incidence of sunlight at particular times of the day and the corresponding reflections are known. It was a long study that was a lot of fun. A kind of meditation on plaster.

DF I am currently teaching at the Düsseldorf Art Academy and trying to understand what it means to teach architecture at an art academy and what role we can play. You teach at the Academy of Fine Arts in Munich. How do you work there, what is your teaching about?

ON I did not study art. The first time I taught at the academy was the longest time I've ever been in an art school. The academy is currently discussing a new statute that will define the objectives of the education. One of the suggestions was that we educate successful artists. That seems to me to be the most absurd thing you could prescribe to an art school as a programme. In addition to the practical work, it is important for me to develop a kind of critical and sensual thinking. It's not just about reflecting on something, but also about tracking it down and making sure how sensuality is formatted. How we change through and in designs, what it means to work artistically.

But perhaps again back to the Bauhaus and Gropius. It fascinates me how the Bauhaus School was established and with what force things were put on their feet. The precision and clarity that took place and made many things possible impress me again and again. It may have been a bit disrespectful at first, but the ability to organize, design and enforce such things impresses me. Gropius has also established a completely different concept of the coexistence of architecture and art. In the end, it was he who dared to include the artists, even at the risk that they would all—figuratively speaking—stab him in the back.

DF Which they in part did, and justifiably so.

ON Whoever wants Caesar also gets Brutus.

DF My interest in Gropius—this may not have been sufficiently appreciated at the beginning—is, of course, also connected with his work as an architect and refers in particular to two of his buildings: the Fagus factory in Alfeld in 1911 and the Bauhaus building in Dessau in 1926. They are two milestones in architecture. But another decisive aspect for me—and that's why I asked about teaching—is the educational concept of the Bauhaus.

In my opinion, bringing together architecture and art, industry and crafts are important factors in building. This is what interests me about the Bauhaus—not the formal expression, but the conceptual approach. The name "Bauhaus" expresses this orientation in an ingenious way.

In teaching, we try to bring artists and architects together and realize real projects one-to-one. Instead of the pure designs that remain ideas, projects are created for real clients. The experience of building opens another dimension.

Normally, we do not manage this moment of translating a concept into a real building at school. But every time I experimented with this realization with my students, something happened, and they approached the projects very differently. So, if there's something that really interests me about Gropius' work, it's the aspect of building. The making as a process and exploration of material that I include in teaching.

I still think this is topical and correct nowadays, and I actually understand it as an important teaching of the Bauhaus.

Donatella Fioretti was born in 1962 in Savona, Italy and studied architecture at the IUAV in Venice and at the University of Kassel. Together with Piero Bruno and José Gutierrez Marquez, she founded the architectural office Bruno Fioretti Marquez in Berlin in 1995. After a guest professorship at the Technical University of Berlin, she worked there as Professor of Building Construction and Design from 2011 to 2017. Since 2017 she has taught as Professor of Architecture at the Düsseldorf Art Academy. In addition to the New Masters' Houses in Dessau, the office's projects include the central library in Berlin Köpenick, 2009, and the Centro Esercizio in Pollegio, 2014.

Olaf Nicolai is an artist who was born in 1962 in Halle an der Saale and who works with various media. He studied German language and literature and received his doctorate from the University of Leipzig in 1992. His work has already been shown in numerous solo and group exhibitions, and he has been awarded several scholarships and prizes, including a scholarship from the German Academy in Rome and the Studienstiftung des deutschen Volkes. Since 2011 he has taught sculpture and three-dimensional design at the Academy of Fine Arts in Munich. In 2014 he designed the interiors of the New Masters' Houses Gropius and Moholy-Nagy in Dessau.

Walter Gropius was born in Berlin in 1883 and died in Boston in 1969. After a non-completed study at the technical universities of Munich and Berlin, he worked with Peter Behrens before he founded his own architecture office in 1910. In 1919 he succeeded Henry van de Velde as director of the School of Arts and Crafts in Weimar and thus became the founder of the Bauhaus in Weimar and, from 1926 on, in Dessau. In 1934 he emigrated to England and later to the USA, where he worked from 1937 as a professor of architecture at Harvard University in Cambridge and as a freelance architect. His many works include the Fagus-Werk in Alfeld an der Leine, 1912, the housing estates Dessau-Törten, 1928, and Karlsruhe Dammerstock, 1929, as well as the main building and the Master's Houses of the Bauhaus in Dessau, 1926.

László Moholy-Nagy was born in Bácsborsód in 1895 and died in Chicago in 1946. After studying law, he devoted himself to painting from 1918. In 1923 he became a teacher at the Bauhaus in Weimar and later in Dessau, where he worked with painting, graphics, photography and film. In 1928 he established a studio in Berlin, but in 1934 emigrated via the Netherlands and England to the USA, where he founded and directed the New Bauhaus in Chicago (later Chicago School of Design) in 1937. He is regarded as an important photogram artist of the 1920s, and his work shaped the aesthetic appearance and marketing of the Bauhaus.

on **Alejandro
de la Sota**

**José Ortega
y Gasset**

T.S. Eliot

**Surrender and
Universality**

The text "Surrender and Universality" is a short-
ened version of the lecture given by Alberto
Campo Baeza on Alejandro de la Sota. Even as
a student, he was fascinated with de la Sota's
work and approach, which he explored from
this time on through excursions into topics related to architecture.

All creative work, including architecture, that is aimed at a greater universality requires a certain degree of depersonalization and objectification. This is what we are told by our protagonists—a poet, a philosopher and an architect.

One might ask oneself, what is the connection between a poet, a philosopher and an architect? What does T. S. Eliot have to do with Ortega y Gasset; and what with Alejandro de la Sota? T. S. Eliot lived from 1888 to 1965. He was born in the United States, but later moved to Britain and wrote poems like an angel. Ortega lived in Spain from 1883 to 1955 and was a clear and transparent Heideggerian. De la Sota lived from 1913 to 1996 and was a laconic, Bachian, Spanish architect.

The three could have known each other as they were contemporaries. If this had been the case, the poet, the philosopher and the architect would have been surprised at what they had in common.

If we were to attribute a single adjective to each of them, we could call T. S. Eliot transparent, Ortega clear and Sota laconic. The similarities between the three can be found in their respective genres—poetry, philosophy and architecture—and in their respective demands for a sobriety of expression, a certain surrender of the individual and a presumed universality.

T. S. ELIOT

In his essays "What is a Classic?" and "Tradition and the Individual Talent", T. S. Eliot stoutly defends the need for the extinction of personality in his work in the interest of greater universality. Already in an older text from 1919, there are many arguments that he continues in the first text of this publication, which is a wonderful speech that he made as President of the Virgil Society of London in 1944.

Eliot writes here: "When an author appears, in his love of the elaborate structure, to have lost the ability to say anything simply; when his addiction to pattern becomes such that he says things elaborately which should properly be said simply, and thus limits his range of expression, the process of complexity ceases to be quite healthy, and the writer is losing touch with the spoken language."[1]

If one exchanges the words author and writer with the term architect, the necessity and qualities of his search for a new simplicity, even a relative roughness in another discipline, become evident.

Alejandro de la Sota
Colegio Maravillas
Madrid 1961

Alejandro de la Sota
Colegio Maravillas
Madrid 1961

To a certain extent, the sacrifice of some potentials for the realization of others is a condition of artistic creation, just as it is a condition of life itself. In short, without the constant application of a classical measure, we tend to become provincial. Furthermore, T. S. Eliot himself uses the term "provincial"; whether this term has the same highly pejorative connotation in English as the word *provinciano* in Spanish, I do not know. Certainly, however, in his search for the universal, he is concerned with avoiding a distortion of values in which what has been added is confused with the essential, what is ephemeral mistaken with the permanent. For him, the progress in the process of artistic creation is a continuous self-abandonment, a continuous annihilation of personality and a search for a balance with tradition. It is also this de-personalization that enables a more objective confrontation with art.

JOSÉ ORTEGA Y GASSET

Ortega writes in his essay "En torno al 'Coloquio de Darmstadt, 1951'": "In effect, style has a very peculiar role in architecture, which it doesn't have in other arts, even in the purer arts. Paradoxical though it may seem, that is how it is. In other arts, style is merely a question of the artist: he decides—with all his being and with a level of decision-making that runs deeper than his will and consequently acquires an aspect of necessity rather than free will—for himself and unto himself. His style does not and cannot depend on anyone else but himself. But the same is not true of architecture. If an architect produces a project with an admirable personal style, he is not, strictly speaking, a good architect."[2]

In 1951 Heidegger and Ortega attended an architectural congress held in Darmstadt. Ortega surprisingly dared to directly criticize this style of individualistic architecture—provincial, in Eliot's words—with great clarity. This makes me think of an extraordinary architect like Antoni Gaudí and of how his excessive individuality took away the universality from his works, the universality we find in masters like Mies van der Rohe or Le Corbusier. Ortega continues with the thesis:

"The architect finds himself in a relationship with his art, very different from the bond formed between other artists and their respective works. The reason for this is obvious: architecture is not, cannot be, must not be an exclusively individual art. It is a collective art. The genuine architect is an entire people, which provide the means of construction, its purpose and its unity. Imagine a city built by amazing, but dedicated architects, each out for himself, and his own individual style. Each one of these buildings could be magnificent, and yet the overall effect would be bizarre and intolerable. In such a scenario, far too much emphasis would be given to an aspect of all art which has not been sufficiently remedied: its capricious element. Its capriciousness would manifest itself naked, cynical, indecent, intolerable. We would not be able to see the building as part of the sovereign objectivity of a great mineral body but displaying, on the contrary, the impertinent profile of someone who is doing whatever he feels like."[3]

It seems that Ortega's words could still be uttered today regarding much of the contradictory, capricious architecture being built.

ALEJANDRO DE LA SOTA

"One tires of seeing beauty and the grace of things (perhaps they are the same) being pursued with added embellishments, knowing the secret is not there. My unforgettable friend J. A. Coderch used to say that ultimate beauty is like a beautiful bald head (Nefertiti, for example), from which one had pulled out each and every hair, lock by lock, with the pain of ripping them out, one by one."[4]

Painfully we have to tear the hairs of our works, which prevent us from reaching their simple, simple end.

These expressive words of the Spanish architect Alejandro de la Sota, who was born in Pontevedra in 1913, are written at the end of his monograph (1990), and define so well the views of this true maestro—who started each day playing a Bach sonata—on his architecture as well as on life itself.

Sota's architecture has this extreme elegance of the precise gesture, the exact sentence that so accurately touches the silence. The silence of his work and his personality had the rare ability to fascinate. Close to poetry, poetic breath, hushed music.

Sota's architecture is specially inscribed in the gymnasium of the Maravillas School in Madrid. This superb building is impressive in its exceptionally terse, pithy and absolute simplicity. This simplicity is such that it does not attract the attention of non-architects, and it is probably difficult for a layman to understand the beauty it contains—and this is for the same reason that it is difficult for them to understand a painting by

Alejandro de la Sota
Gobierno Civil
Tarragona 1957

Mark Rothko. This simplicity of the most logical architecture led Sota to say, "I believe that not making architecture is a way of making it."
Thinking a little further, we could hear Sota say that architecture is not a free expression of emotion, but an escape from emotion, which is exactly what T. S. Eliot wrote about poetry. Or as my old friend Konstantin Stepanovich Melnikov put it, "Having become my own boss, I entreated architecture to throw off her gown of marble, remove her make-up and reveal herself as she really is: like a goddess, naked, graceful and young. And to renounce being agreeable and compliant, as befits true beauty." [5]
How could we fail to recognize the identical universal nature in our three protagonists? As the years go by, I must acknowledge the great intellectual pleasure that the interaction of these three characters and their themes brings to my memory. How great and productive is the passage of time?

1   T. S. Eliot, *What is a classic?* (London: Faber & Faber, 1945), 16.

2   Translation by the author: José Ortega y Gasset, "En torno al 'Coloquio de Darmstadt, 1951'", in *Meditación de la técnica y otros ensayos sobre ciencia y filosofía* (Madrid: Alianza Editorial, 2004), 110–111.

3   Translation by the author: José Ortega y Gasset, "En torno al 'Coloquio de Darmstadt, 1951'", in *Meditación de la técnica y otros ensayos sobre ciencia y filosofía* (Madrid: Alianza Editorial, 2004), 110–111.

4   Translation by the author: Alejandro de la Sota, *Alejandro de la Sota, architect* (Madrid: Pronaos, 1989), back cover.

5   S. Frederick Starr, *Melnikov: Solo Architect in a Mass Society* (New Jersey: Princeton University Press, 1978), 117.

Alejandro de la Sota
Gobierno Civil
Tarragona 1957

Alberto Campo Baeza was born in Valladolid in 1946 and studied architecture at the Universidad Politécnica in Madrid. He has been a professor of architecture there since 1986 and also works as an architect. He has taught at ETH Zurich, EPF in Lausanne, Pennsylvania University in Philadelphia, Kansas State University and Vienna University of Technology. In 2017 he was appointed to the renowned Clarkson Chair of Architecture at the University of Buffalo. His works have been awarded numerous prizes, including the Heinrich Tessenow Gold Medal and the Piranesi Prix di Roma. Campo Baeza is a member of the RIBA International Fellowship and the Honorary Fellowship of the American Institute of Architects (AIA) as well as an academic member of the Real Academia de Bellas Artes de San Fernando. His works include the Museo de la Memoria in Granada, 2009, the office building of the Junta de Castilla y León in Zamora, 2011, and the Casa del Infinito in Cadiz, 2014.

Alejandro de la Sota Martínez was born in Pontevedra in 1913 and died in Madrid in 1996. After studying architecture in Madrid, he founded his own architectural practice. From 1956 to 1972 he was also a professor at the Universidad Politécnica of Madrid. His works include the Gobierno Civil in Tarragona, 1957, the Maravillas School in Madrid, 1961, and the Pavillón Municipal dos Deportes in Pontevedra, 1966.

José Ortega y Gasset was born in Madrid in 1883 and died there in 1955. He studied philosophy at the University of Deusto in Bilbao and at the Complutense University of Madrid, where he received his doctorate in 1904. After studying in Germany, he was appointed Professor of Psychology, Logic and Ethics at the Escuela Superior del Magisterio de Madrid in 1908 and Full Professor of Metaphysics at the Complutense University in Madrid in 1910. He founded the Liga de Educación Política Española, 1914, the magazine *España*, 1915, and co-founded the newspaper *Sol*, 1916. His works include the publications *España invertebrada*, 1921, *El tema de nuestro tiempo*, 1923, and *La rebelión de las masas*, 1930.

Thomas Stearns Eliot was born in 1888 in St. Louis, Missouri and died in 1965 in London. He studied philosophy and literature at Harvard University. He moved to England in 1914 and became a British citizen in 1927. There, he worked as a poet, essayist, playwright, and literary and social critic, but also as a publisher. In 1948 he was awarded the Nobel Prize for Literature. Among his most famous works are the lyrical works *The Waste Land*, 1922, *The Hollow Men*, 1925, *Ash Wednesday*, 1930, and *Four Quartets*, 1943. His plays also became famous, especially *Murder in the Cathedral*, 1935, and *The Cocktail Party*, 1950.

on Francesco Borromini

with Stephan Trüby

The lecture and the subsequent discussion by Christian Kerez and Stephan Trüby on Francesco Borromini illuminate the possible echo, continuity of content and intellectual similarities between Borromini's and Kerez's work.

`ST` The mention of Borromini as one of your role models surprised me. Because if I put your work in relation to the old opposition of Bernini versus Borromini, law versus emotion, I would assign it to the element of law. Does this reference to Borromini exist because he is so distant from you?

`CK` In our time, more than ever before, anything is possible in formal and technical terms. I try to find rules to understand architecture as a discipline again. That's why I'm interested in law in the sense of a set of rules.

I'm very interested in the approach of defining something not through individual design preferences but through rules of the game, through abstract correlations such as structures in contrast to fixed architectural formations. In this context, I also see Borromini as someone who uses a conventional set of rules and transfers it into a new context, breaks it up and explores how far these rules can make something new possible without losing credibility. For me, he is not a subversive or mannerist who, like Guarini or Bernini, celebrated the decline or overcoming of the architectural style elements of classicism in their sculptural fountains, but someone who continues existing laws and pushes them to their limits. He extends a vocabulary of forms beyond the state of the time.

`ST` We will talk selectively about the reception of Borromini in the twentieth century using three examples. Paolo Portoghesi, in his own view, depicts Borromini as a fantastic cabinetmaker who did not follow the classical rules to the same extent as Bernini and others. Robert Venturi and Denise Scott Brown, who saw in him a guarantor of complexity and contradiction in architecture, gave another interpretation of his oeuvre.

I would like to present a third point of view with an excursus on the space of the unique staircase in Palazzo Barberini by Borromini.

I experienced this space for the very first time when I came to Rome from London in the late 1990s, from a place where everyone discussed parametric design before it was called parametric design, and then suddenly in Italy I was confronted with this Baroque staircase made of multiple curved surfaces. I began to puzzle over not only how this room had been built but how it had been conceived. How did it go for you?

CK   I was overwhelmed too. This extremely small room is basically just one chamber in this great palace, one hall among many, yet it unites one of the most elementary architectural contradictions.

One could say that the canon of classical architecture is based on horizontal and vertical lines. But this small room already completely violates this very first, fundamental, architectural description of a classicist vocabulary. All the elements of the architecture are taken diagonally upwards here, not in a dizzying, daring way, but, on the contrary, very carefully and quite naturally to eliminate contradictions. The rigid sides and roof cornices are turned and moved without effort. One can see this very beautifully, for example, in the detail of how the supports stand on the deep stair railing that winds up in the stairwell. Each support gets an additional base area, which is rounded and follows the railing completely; it expands. The forces are first gradually transferred into the horizontal by the ascending movement and only then, one could say when on safe ground, are they transferred into supports.

The already familiar is thought out of a completely new context and, in this sense, our perception is expanded.

ST   Let us come back to the reception by Paolo Portoghesi, who, as for example a comparison of the Fontana Chapel with the Casa Baldi of Portoghesi shows, has dealt with Borromini in his very own way. What insights did you gain about Borromini in your confrontation with this protagonist of the twentieth century?

CK   Portoghesi is an architect I like very much. I also met him personally and visited him at his house outside Rome. Through drawing, he found a representation, a reception and an analytical instrument for systems, which, at the same time, served him as a design tool. Through the drawings of the undulating curves of the friezes and columns in Borromini's churches, he directly finds his own building designs. Through graphic analysis, he created an independent work in strong contrast to the many other, much more striking buildings of postmodernism, but also in contrast to the inflationary method of working with references that is now widespread.

ST   At this point, I dare to reduce your architectural oeuvre to two images. In other words, the previous oeuvre complet by Christian Kerez, to be shown in thirty seconds. This short story begins with the chapel St Nepomuk, your first work, and finds its relative end in the installation *Incidental Space* at the Venice Biennale. My thesis is that Borromini is in this evolution from building one to the project in Venice.

CK   These two buildings are very related. For me, they're actually the same in different forms. In the most elementary, shortest form in which I can describe both, it's an isolated interior room that also appears as a body to the outside. The two buildings show a brute relationship between inside and outside that is rarely possible in architecture today. This principle connects both buildings more in my understanding of architecture than their form distinguishes them from each other.
If one understands architecture from the work on spaces and derives it exclusively from the interior of the buildings, one must at some point nevertheless show what all these interior spaces look like from the outside. This is a painful moment for me because I am not particularly interested in the external appearance of a house. In the meantime, I have found many tricks for avoiding this step, so that many of my buildings no longer have an exterior but only an interior. *Incidental Space* has created a space in which inside and outside are identical. But this contribution to the Biennale is also, as you say, a tribute to Borromini.
I got to know Borromini very late in my life, two years before the *Incidental Space* was designed. I love certain spaces and certain buildings immediately, unrestrictedly and without firm intentions. Not with the ulterior motive of my own use, a transfer into my own designs. It is only through this direct emotion that they can influence designs indirectly and completely unconsciously.
The fact that an influence arises from this emotion means that it has nothing in common with a method or even only with a conscious reference. I never thought of Borromini during the whole design or construction phase. Only later, through my good friend Smiljan Radic, did I realize that there could be a connection here. But a homage is something completely different than a literal or alienated use of a historical model. The subsequent attempt at rationalization is perhaps only a con-

sequence of talking about what one likes to look at, and perhaps one doesn't even want to understand why one is moved infinitely more by one space than by another.

ST   For today's discussion, I brought with me some stages between these two buildings, the chapel and the Swiss Pavilion, which were originally intended to support my thesis that Borromini is reflected like a leitmotif in certain elements of your works. But now you've pulled the rug out from under my feet when you said that you only got to know Borromini two years before this pavilion.

However, I still believe that there is a reference to Borromini's work and to the themes that you were only able to name later in his work, and I would like to talk about another building of yours at this point. In your analysis of Borromini, you just emphasized the theme of wholeness and spoke of an architecture that tries to leave elements behind. I'm now asking especially curiously, as someone who was involved in a project called *Elements of Architecture*, if elemental thinking in architecture is something you're trying to leave behind. I'm also thinking here of your project House with One Wall.

CK   All three floors of this building are distinguished from each other by a central wall that is declined in different ways and, at the same time, connected by this elementary, constant principle of space division. The wall initially runs unevenly; legend has it that its course eludes the control and consciousness of the architect. Above it follows a floor in which it receives the minimal bend permitted by the structural engineer; it is almost straight. Finally, at the top it jumps deep into and out of the room to accommodate the niches for the bathroom.

By examining a single architectural element, the building is not defined by several similarly folded walls, as it might have been in an initial design approach, but by walls that, in their diversity, take us to extremes and relate to one another. At the same time, the building becomes a unit, not as a design unit, as the sum of walls and slabs, but through a staircase that runs along this wall, leading the visitor in and out. It stretches from one end of the building to the other and from the lowest to the highest floor so that an actual, tangible fusion is created between the three piled-up, bent wall panels via the height development. This unity can be experienced through the radical

reduction of architectural elements. This wall is both supporting structure, installation shaft and the only spatial definition
of the two apartments and leads the stairs from the entrance
directly to the top floor.
This tendency to differentiate architectural elements in their
appearance to the extreme in order to break their generic character and thus define them more as part of an overall context
can be found in all of Borromini's buildings. It differs fundamentally from many examples of contemporary architecture,
where details speak for themselves and enrich the architecture
as gadgets without emerging from it.

> ST   Another important stage in your work is the well-known
> Leutschenbach School in Zurich. Quite obviously an architec-
> ture of wholeness, which also consists of parts. Can you use this
> example to explain the dialectic of parts and the whole that par-
> ticularly fascinates you about Borromini?

CK   There are two areas where the trusses are visible from
the outside—at the top of the gym and along the three-storey
classroom wing. This is further subdivided by balconies. In
terms of height, there is certainly comparability between this
section of the building with three levels and the very high top
floor. If you take a closer look, you can see that the trusses are
a bit different, that they become narrower at the top because
they are connected to the facade structure there, while at the
bottom they are oriented to the subdivision of the rooms. I was
very interested in this diversity, but at the same time in this
reference across the public floors, where the trusses can only
be experienced from the inside. It is not a building in which
almost every section is designed independently, where stack-
ing is more like a collage, but an attempt to form a higher unity,
a complex unity.
This differentiation of the steel trusses from the respective
conditions also leads, for example, to the fact that the entire
building does not stand on a truss but on six tripod-like supports, because the weights that are transferred here exceed all
possible lateral forces such as earthquakes or wind forces. Not
only does the cohesion between the individual struts change
between one storey and the next, but also the structure of the
struts themselves, their width and the plate thickness of the
plates welded together from high-performance steel only for

this construction change extremely according to their static load. The systemic cohesion of the individual elements of the building is shown here in a way naked, as a supporting structure, while the architectural elements of Borromini are just as systemically differentiated but almost always remain a plastic design of the wall.

ST Another of your buildings that is not yet so well known is a villa in Prague that is currently under construction. It will be the home of a prominent, perhaps one may say politically controversial Czech politician. Can we perhaps imagine here a kind of echo of the play of convex and concave spaces as we know them from Borromini?

CK This house is a kind of antithesis to the houses I have built so far. It reflects the attempt to create width, spatial expansion not through a single large space, not through standardization, but, on the contrary, through a multiplication of spaces. The geometry of the floor plan is based on slightly overlapping circles. There are open spaces, consisting of several circular chambers that are connected without doors and are supplemented by closed interspaces that have doors. There is the space within these circles, but also the space between these circles. A hierarchical system was created, with main and secondary rooms, with connected physical, cylindrical rooms and closed, narrow, fragmentary interspaces. There are, simultaneously, the concave integral open spaces within the circular geometries and the convex fragmentary closed spaces outside and between these perfect spaces.

In the church of St Ivo, the same theme of linking concave and convex wall sections can be found in a completely different form. One could describe St Ivo as a series of niches that extend the space, followed by intruding building elements. And just as these opposing spatial forms in this central space are inextricably linked to each other, so they also face each other again and again because of their uneven number. In St Ivo, space-expanding wall sections, concave and convex forms, opposites, inextricably merge into a single space.

ST The floor plans are reminiscent of the famous Russian Orthodox Basilius Cathedral on Red Square in Moscow. Is there any connection or is it coincidence?

CK For me, this project in Prague wouldn't have existed without working on a favela in Brazil. This also shows that architectural themes have a lasting effect beyond political or social connections. It was the experience of working on the favela, an atomized city, a city that lives from the small-scale and multiplication, from a composite, additive character that was important for the rules of this project.

This immense mass of bricks, which is the result of the small-scale nature of the construction method, in its geometric stringency does indeed awaken a certain resemblance to ancient buildings. First of all, I thought about structures of Roman antiquity, but only during my last visit to the building site.

ST Another building is the lake-view house in Zurich where there is an interesting moment, the very focused, cave-like perspective of Lake Zurich. I would like to compare this with a work by Borromini, the famous Galleria Spada, in the Palazzo Spada in Rome. It is about a trick of perspective. The sculpture, which can be seen at the very end of this corridor, measures only one meter but appears life-size.

CK I find the comparison, which would never have occurred to me, very interesting. The title "House with a Lake View" sounds trivial and most architects would, if they built a house in a place that allows a beautiful view of the lake, come up with the idea of giving this view free and planning a large glazed area, but a lake view on a favoured slope always implies looking down. This idea leads to the broken geometry of the roof shape. A gabled roof, which makes maximum use of the property, also follows the inclination of the slope with its ridge, creating a non-tectonic, therefore rather cave-like roof, which leads down to the view of the lake. There is no horizontal view. I think that this inclined orientation is very dominant in this room, but also in the apartments below. It's a loft, one could also say its a bit banal, but the interesting thing about it is that the view is turned down, as if the loft were in an inclined position. This diagonality is much stronger than the openness and size of the room. This gives the room a feeling of falling, similar to the perspective built in Palazzo Spada, which also collapses the passage to a garden in a certain way, in height and width, to lead into the seemingly endless depth.

Francesco Borromini
Sant'Ivo alla Sapienza
Rome 1642–1660

Francesco Borromini
Sant'Ivo alla Sapienza
Rome 1642–1660

ST   In recent works, such as your project in Guangzhou, you seem to leave your architectural beginnings completely behind. At the same time as you were working on the Swiss Pavilion in Venice in 2016, you moved your head office from Switzerland to Berlin. Only the ancillary office is now in Zurich. Is dealing with free forms and convex, concave and complex spaces an attempt to leave Zurich behind you to a certain extent?

CK   I never tried to leave Zurich behind me. It's more of a spurned love. I tried harder than anywhere else to win competitions, but I was completely unsuccessful. And, of course, this lack of success is hard to bear if you know the background and who wins which competition for what reason. In China, I'm just as unsuccessful because I haven't won a single competition yet, but at least I don't know why I lose a competition and that involves a moment of intellectual freedom. I think there is nothing worse than knowing how to win a competition and then to do it. It is amazing how, in one of the oldest democracies in the world, competition is enslaved and misappropriated and, at the same time, in a country governed politically by a single party, there is competition that leaves everything open. In China, the programme is often only half written, the payment is always very decent and you have complete freedom. If you then really want to win and know how to do it, you probably won't make such drafts as we do. In this sense, this freedom may be deceptive. I left Switzerland because I know it too well. In addition, the degree of freedom in competition has increased, and, mirroring this, public architectural debates have deteriorated dramatically in recent years, which is making Switzerland less attractive.

ST   Your farewell gift to Switzerland, to Zurich, is the already mentioned Swiss Pavilion from 2016 at the Architecture Biennale in Venice, which probably explains most clearly why the debate with Borromini was considered. Could you explain this?

CK   The significance of a building cannot be derived from its size. But what fascinated me about the large scale and why I turned to China was the hope of developing buildings with great architectural complexity, because a set of rules unleashes completely different possibilities on a large scale than on a small one.

The projects in China were not based on forms, but on rules about how to develop these forms in the first place. This interest in the basic rules of architecture links the projects in China with the projects I used to design in Switzerland. In the same sense, one could say that this search for complexity, which is linked to it, continues in the same sense in the pavilion for the Venice Biennale, but with Swiss possibilities, that is, with an extremely modest space programme.

With my contribution to the Biennale, I attempted to change the size effect of the spatial installation, which covers only twenty-five square metres. The space appears to be much larger than it actually is. Borromini's rooms usually have modest dimensions, but they seem almost infinitely large and complex.

In the San Carlo alle Quattro Fontane church, the distance from the entrance portal to the altar is extremely short. At the same time, the eye is so strongly occupied by the niches, which, between the evenly arranged supports, extend the space in various ways and lead the view in different directions, that the short path across the actual space extends in several directions and in different ways. This is not to mention the development of this space in its height, where, over arch-like niches, the view leads into a perspective-shortened dome space and across it into a skylight room with a ceiling painting. This creates a magnificent expanse in this small building, which is modest in itself.

ST The reactions to the Swiss Pavilion were very rapid; both the archaics and the parametricians reacted euphorically to this space. Can you say something about the reactions from your perspective on this room?

CK In the Swiss Pavilion I had the opportunity to explain to Patrik Schumacher, who once found the contribution terrible, that this space represents the future of parametric design. A robot has unlimited possibilities to do something. But if you let computers or robots do everything, then just until recently you would have had problems with the storage capacities during the calculations. That's why most forms in parametric design were created with comparatively simple computer programs,

Francesco Borromini
San Carlo alle Quattro Fontane
Rome 1638–1641

Francesco Borromini
San Carlo alle Quattro Fontane
Rome 1638–1641

which, through the resulting aesthetics, in turn led to a proximity to art nouveau, to Louis Sullivan and to other architects
who actually worked with very simple geometric means. The
storage space required for our project would not have existed
five years ago.

ST We have been discussing Borromini's architecture and
your architecture, but we haven't talked about Borromini as
a person yet. There are some representations of Borromini's
life that are characterized by ruptures and tragedies. He com-
mitted suicide, and there is a rumour that he was a murderer.
He supposedly threw an employee off the roof of a construction site.
My question to you would be, is a fascination for the buildings of Borromini also a fascination for the man Borromini, a
man who lived a transgressive life? Perhaps on a professional
level?

CK This story about throwing a man off a roof hundreds
of years ago, which I have never heard of, would be difficult
to prove today, as would proving it to be untrue. But the suicide is understandable. Borromini was seriously ill at the end of
his life, and the doctors gave him a phosphorus tincture to take
orally for recovery. The medical healing practices of that time
were often pure torture with no great prospect of recovery.
I know very little about the man Borromini, and I have to say
that even if I knew more, I don't know if it would affect the
enjoyment or experience of his architecture. I'm not really
interested in the person Borromini at all. I will never be able to
meet him myself. Even if it turned out that Borromini was, in
fact, a pseudonym for a collective of designers, this would not
change my personal encounter with his work.
Although in Borromini's case, there are understandable reasons for his suicide, the current reception of his work constantly
establishes a link between his work and his suicide, in contrast to
Mark Rothko, for instance, who does not draw any connections
between his suicide and his work. The reason for Borromini's
suicide is not understandable from his work; he had completely
different fateful, comprehensible reasons. Borromini's architectural work has an almost incomprehensible complexity. In
it, opposites unceasingly combine and merge completely and
seamlessly into one another. It is probably the inconceivability

of the work that leads art historians to draw pseudo-psycholog-
ical speculations for its explanation. Their scientific approach
is doomed to failure in view of the great, unleashed character
of his spatial experience.
In architecture, the work is the only essential thing.

Christian Kerez was born in 1962 in Venezuela. After a large number of publications in the field of architectural photography, he opened his own architectural office in Zurich in 1993. Kerez has held a full professorship at the Swiss Federal Institute of Technology Zurich since 2009, following his previous appointments as visiting and assistant professor. From 2012 to 2013, he held the Kenzo Tange Chair at Harvard University in Cambridge. In 2016 he participated in the Swiss Pavilion at the Architecture Biennale in Venice. Among his works are House with One Wall in Zurich, completed in 2007, the schoolhouse Leutschenbach in Zurich, completed in 2009, and the Porto Seguro Housing Development Project in Sao Paulo, which was developed from 2009 to 2013.

Stephan Trüby, born in 1970 in Stuttgart, teaches as a senior professor at the IGMA, Institute for the Fundamentals of Modern Architecture and Design at the University of Stuttgart. Other important academic positions have included a visiting professorship in architecture at the Staatliche Hochschule für Gestaltung in Karlsruhe, 2007–2009, the management of the postgraduate study programme "Spatial Design" at the Zurich University of the Arts, 2009–2014, his work as a lecturer at the Graduate School of Design at Harvard University, 2012–2014, and an assistant professorship at the Technical University of Munich, 2014–2018. He was research director of the Architecture Biennale Venice 2014 and is a permanent contributor to the journals *ARCH+* and *Archithese*. His publications include *Geschichte des Korridors,* 2018, as author, and *architektur_theorie.doc*, 2003, and *Elements of Architecture*, 2014, as co-editor.

Francesco Borromini was born as Francesco Castelli in 1599 in Bissone and died in 1667 in Rome. Trained as a stonemason in Milan, he worked from 1619 under his later rival Gian Lorenzo Bernini at St Peter's in Rome. As a representative of the Roman Baroque, he developed an individual style and built the San Carlo alle Quattro Fontane in Rome from 1638 to 1641, the oratorio of St Philip Neri in Rome from 1637 to 1652 and Sant'Ivo alla Sapienza in Rome from 1640 to 1650.

Appendix

Credits
Thanks
Imprint

CREDITS

Page 17
□: Daniel Reh

Pages 18 – 33
Cover□: Daniel Reh
□1: gta Archiv/ETH Zurich,
Ernst Gisel, Fritz Maurer
□2: gta Archiv/ETH Zurich,
Ernst Gisel, Fritz Maurer
□3: Lederer Ragnarsdóttir
Oei, Architekten
□4: Okänd/Arkitektur
och designcentrum/
ARKM.1973-103-084-035
□5: Okänd/Arkitektur
och designcentrum/
ARKM.1973-103-084-044

Pages 34 – 55
Cover□: Uli Benz
□1: Wikipedia/Stefan Flöper
licensed under the Creative
Commons Attribution-
Share-Alike 3.0 license
□2: Ungers Archiv für
Architekturwissenschaft
□3: Ungers Archiv für
Architekturwissenschaft

Pages 56 – 69
Cover□: Daniel Reh
□1: Marc Rochkind
licensed under the Creative
Commons Attribution-
ShareAlike 4.0 International
license
□2: Monika Sosnowska,
Tower, 2014
Steel, paint, 131 ×
1269 × 263 inches
© Monika Sosnowska,
Courtesy the artist and
Hauser & Wirth
Photocredit: Juliusz
Sokolowski

□3: Monika Sosnowska
Tower, 2014
Steel, paint, 131 ×
1269 × 263 inches
© Monika Sosnowska
Courtesy the artist and
Hauser & Wirth
Photocredit: Juliusz
Sokolowski
□4: Julian Wagner

Pages 70 – 89
Cover□: Daniel Reh
□1: Louis I. Kahn Collection,
University of Pennsylvania
and Pennsylvania Historical
and Museum Commission
□2: Louis I. Kahn Collection,
University of Pennsylvania
and Pennsylvania
Historical and
Museum Commission
□3: Ignacio Paricio
licensed under the Creative
Commons Attribution-
NonCommercial-
ShareAlike 3.0 Unported
license
□4: seier+seier
licensed under the Creative
Commons Attribution 2.0
Generic license

Pages 90 – 105
Cover□: Daniel Reh
□1: Torben Eskerod
□2: Torben Eskerod
□3: Alastair Philip Wiper
-VIEW/Alamy
□4: Jens Markus Lindhe

Pages 106 – 125
Cover□: Daniel Reh
□1: Ford Motor Company
Collection, Gift of Ford
Motor Company and John C.
Waddell, 1987

□2: Bauhaus-Archiv Berlin/
©VG Bild-Kunst, Bonn 2019
□3: Bauhaus-Archiv Berlin/
©VG Bild-Kunst, Bonn 2019
□4: Olaf Nicolai, *Le pigment
de la lumière, Studie 8*,
2014
White gouache on Ingres
paper, 63,2 × 48,5 cm
Courtesy Galerie EIGEN +
ART Leipzig/Berlin,
Photo: Uwe Walter, Berlin,
VG Bild-Kunst, Bonn 2019

Pages 126 – 137
Cover□: Daniel Reh
□1: Fundación Alejandro de
la Sota, Alejandro de la Sota
□2: Fundación Alejandro de
la Sota, Alejandro de la Sota
□3: Fundación Alejandro de
la Sota, Alejandro de la Sota
□4: Fundación Alejandro de
la Sota, Alejandro de la Sota

Pages 138 – 155
Cover□: Uli Benz
□1: Christian Kerez
□2: Christian Kerez
□3: Christian Kerez
□4: Christian Kerez

THANKS

Our thanks go first and foremost to the architects who, as part of the *Architects on Architects* series of events, spoke about the influence of role models from the history of architecture on their work. We also wish to thank the interlocutors from the fields of fine arts, journalism and architectural theory. A big thank you goes to the Department of Architecture for its generous support of the lecture series, which was held in connection with the 150th anniversary of the Technical University of Munich. We would like to thank all the members of staff, especially those from the Chair of Urban Architecture and the Chair of Architectural Design and Conception at the Technical University of Munich, for their contribution to the series and the countless steps necessary to make this book possible.

For their generous financial support, we would like to thank:

– The Department of Architecture,
  Technical University of Munich
– designfunktion – Gesellschaft für moderne Einrichtung mbH
– Vitra International AG
– Grohe Deutschland Vertriebs GmbH
– designerwerkschau
– Investa Real Estate
– Franz Schneider Brakel GmbH + Co KG
– Keimfarben GmbH
– Kristalia Srl

IMPRINT

Editors
Dietrich Fink, Uta Graff,
Nils Rostek, Julian Wagner

TUM

Technical University of
Munich
Chair of Urban Architecture
Chair of Architectural
Design and Conception

Publisher
Hirmer Verlag
Bayerstrasse 57–59
80335 Munich

www.hirmerpublishers.com

Translation
Nils Rostek, Julian Wagner,
Munich

Copy-editing and
proofreading
Owen Connors, Munich

Design
2×Goldstein, Rheinstetten

Lithography and prepress
Reproline mediateam GmbH
& Co. KG

Printing and binding
Kösel GmbH & Co. KG

Paper
Munken Print White 115 g/m2
Chromolux Metallic Silver
250 g/m2

Font
Theinhardt, Lyon Text

Printed in Germany

Bibliographic information
of the Deutsche National-
bibliothek
The Deutsche National-
bibliothek lists this publication in the Deutsche
Nationalbibliografie; detailed
bibliographic data are
available on the Internet at
http://dnb.de.

© 2019 Hirmer Verlag GmbH,
Munich; the authors.

ISBN 978-3-7774-3308-0